PARETO'S REPUBLIC
AND THE NEW SCIENCE OF PEACE

FILIP PALDA

Date of issue: December 2011.
Printed and bound in Canada by the Gilmore Press.

Published by Cooper-Wolfling. None of the advisory board of Cooper-Wolfling are responsible for the opinions expressed in this text, which remain the responsibility of the author.

Editor: J. Kristin McCahon
Typesetting and final design supervisor: Lindsey Thomas Martin
Proofreader: Mirja van Herk
Cover design and typesetting: Gibaudrac Studios

About the cover: The cover is an image derived from the Evgeniy Vuchetich sculpture Let Us Beat Swords into Plowshares donated by the Soviet Union to the United Nations in New York in 1959. The derived image is used with the written permission of the legal division of the United Nations.

Palda, Filip, 1962–
Pareto's Republic / Filip Palda.
Includes bibliographical references.
ISBN 978-0-9877880-3-0

THIS BOOK IS CERTIFIED TO BE SUBSIDY FREE. NOT ONE DOLLAR
OF TAXPAYER MONEY HAS GONE INTO ITS PRODUCTION.
WWW.PARETOREPUBLIC.COM

About the author

FILIP PALDA IS full professor at the École nationale d'administration publique. He earned his Ph.D. in economics at the University of Chicago under the supervision of Nobel Prize winner Gary Becker. He is the author of six books, the editor of a further six, and has written hundreds of newspaper and magazine articles as well as over twenty-five articles in refereed academic journals. He is a high-scoring author on the RepEc website of economic working papers and is best known for his work on exposing the self-interest politicians hold in crafting election finance laws and for his role in bringing to light and giving the first full theoretical treatment of the displacement deadweight loss of tax evasion, minimum wage evasion, and rent-seeking.

Dedication

PRO MEMU OTCI.

CONTENTS

Acknowledgments

I THANK MY father Kristian Palda who commented on several drafts of this book. His qualifications are particularly suited to giving feedback on a work of this sort. He received his Ph.D. in business at the University of Chicago under Nobel Prize winning economist George Stigler, and Harry Roberts, the founding statistician of marketing in business. My father then won the *Ford Foundation Prize* for original dissertations. He discovered the now famous Lydia Pinkham database which allowed him to prove that advertising could have cumulative effects and from this discovery he showed how to measure the value that advertising can contribute to a firm. This and other discoveries made him a leading figure in business economics. Yet he also has a second, very particular qualification, which is that he grew up first under German occupation forces during their reign of terror in Europe and Russia, and after the liberation of his country, Czechoslovakia, was chased from law school, dispossessed of all he owned, and then chased from his country by fellow students-become-collaborator and other home-grown communists acting with the backing of Russian arms. This has given him a unique perspective on conflict, personal separation, corruption, and absolute power, and one which I have drawn upon extensively in writing this book.

I thank Dan Usher for his detailed comments. Professor Usher received his Ph.D. in economics at the University of Chicago and went on to make foundational contributions first to development economics and then to the theory of tax evasion and deadweight loss, including what I believe is the first discussion of displacement deadweight loss. In a burst of creativity he also founded the field of the dynamics of predation in economic systems, which he called dynastic cycles. I believe though that his most enduring contribution to political economy will be his idea that there are economic prerequisites to democracy. The elegance of his analyses is without peer.

I thank Leonard Dudley, a founder along with Claude Montmarquette of the economic analysis of foreign aid, who provided invaluable comments on my views about economic development. Professor Dudley wrote the sort of book which inspired this one. It is called *The Pen and The Sword* published by Basil Blackwell and is an example of how economic reasoning can rise above economics to become accessible to anyone with the requisite curiosity. Thanks also to Alexandre Couture-Gagnon for her detailed comments.

I thank Kristin McCahon for her invaluable help as editor, proof-reader, and advisor in all matters relating to bringing a book to press. Kristin has for over twenty years been the director of publication production at the Fraser Institute in Vancouver and has been deeply involved in the publishing industry there. Without her patient guidance and brilliant conceptual and detail editing this book simply would not have been possible. Thank you Kristin. Any remaining errors are mine alone! Thanks are also due to Mirja van Herk for final copy-editing and to Lindsey Thomas Martin for supervising the typesetting of this book as well as cover design and dealing with all matters relating to ensuring the manuscript would be fit to send to the printers as well as to Dezso Vaghy for early suggestions on cover design. And finally but not least I thank Jim McIntyre, of the Gilmore Press.

USER GUIDE 1

THIS BOOK CAN BE READ from start to finish because it has a uniting theme: Pareto efficiency as a recipe for peace. It has also been designed so that you can go to any page and start learning ideas in economics, political science, and Public Choice theory, because everything in this book relates to some important idea in one or all of these fields.

The book's main idea

ONLY A PEACE that is based on Pareto efficiency, implemented through private property rights, can lead to prosperity and respect for human rights in large societies. What is Pareto efficiency? Some people have heard of something called the Pareto 80-20 rule which says that eighty percent of the profits go to twenty percent of the people. Pareto was a multi-genius, spawning ideas in statistics, sociology, demography, and economics that came to dominate the field. But the 80-20 rule has nothing to do with his notion of efficiency. Pareto efficiency is a much more powerful and subtle concept. A division of resources in society is Pareto-efficient if the pie cannot be re-cut in such a way as to improve the lot of at least one person whilst not making others worse off. This whole book is devoted to exploring this seemingly simple but devastatingly powerful definition of economic efficiency.

Extended summary

A SOCIETY STANDS or falls depending on whether its members feel they are getting as much out of it as they are putting in. Social accounting is the vital ingredient of a successful society; the kind of accounting that creates balance between the efforts people make and the benefits they receive. Societies that get the social accounting right are both rich and peaceful.

By peaceful, I mean a condition in which people within those societies cannot arbitrarily coerce each other. If I cannot force others to do something or give me something that I want, I must find another way to convince them to part with something they own, which I can do by offering them something of mine to which they attach a greater value. Persuasion is a viable basis for balance—and peaceful relations—in all human interactions. And to compound the benefits, persuasion is the source of riches. Riches, in this case, means finding new and better ways of using resources, finding new ways to do old things more efficiently. Studies overwhelming support the view that societies based on voluntary consensus are the most prosperous.

That is the big picture. The book also explains how to achieve Pareto efficiency in practice. Because the essence of Pareto efficiency is the way resources are used, the book explains the two the methods available for allocating their use. Either you can centralize control of resources by putting them under the direction of some organization such as the government, or you can allow individuals to decide how to use resources by letting people own property and decide for themselves what to do with it. The decentralized option works best because it forces people to reveal their true preferences and their abilities, which is the basis of balanced social accounting. The truth emerges from competition. When consumers compete with each other to buy some product, they reveal how much they are willing to pay. When producers lower their prices to beat their competitors, they reveal how low their costs really are.

The ideas in this book are by no means the consensus position. Some serious thinkers have argued that the centralized version of resource control—coercion—not persuasion, is the source of prosperity and peace. Communists believe that a dictatorship of the proletariat can organize things so that people who put in their time at the metal press can go home to a pleasantly chilled bottle of Slivovic. However, to get social accounting right, coercive systems must rely on the wisdom and honesty of their leaders. The paradox is that the one mechanism that could ensure a functional level of both ingredients is not feasible in a state that controls all resources. Democracy is the only feasible check on the venality of rulers because it is the governmental analogue of competition in the private sector. By putting all of society's resources under the control of government, democracy becomes a contest between interest groups to divide the riches of the state, a situation that leads ultimately to civil war.

This book shows how property rights balance social accounts, but also shows that sometimes property rights themselves cannot be established. When this is the case, government must intervene. The proper balance between government and private property rights is the main quest of this book.

Principal components of this book's main idea

SOCIAL ACCOUNTS ARE a tally of the efforts people make in society and the rewards they receive. When these accounts tip too far out of balance, then strife, and possibly the dissolution of that society are the result. This is why a robust system of social accounts is needed to ensure peace in society. This book explains how to get such peace through the exchange of property rights in markets where individuals make choices about the use of private resources. The foundation of the peaceful use of resources is something called Pareto efficiency. An exchange is Pareto-improving if it increases the well-being of at least one person without harming anyone else. When all such exchanges have been made, a society is considered Pareto-efficient.

Pareto efficiency can be attained only if there is an established system of rules that protect private property rights. Such a system ensures that every party to an exchange of resources takes into full account the preferences of the opposite party before the exchange takes place. This ensures balance in social accounts. Governments can serve as useful interveners when property rights and voluntary exchange break down as a means for social accounting.

Outline of the book by chapter

CHAPTER TWO INTRODUCES the idea of peace as a form of managed war. This book is not about changing people. It is about changing something much more amenable to alteration, namely, the environment in which people live. Given the right setting, such as one in which people can resolve their disputes peacefully by exchanging property rights according to rules that are the same for all, prosperity and an effective, if not necessarily loving peace, may result. The chapter introduces the ideas of Vilfredo Pareto, who conceived of such a system of voluntary exchanges that, when executed perfectly, have come to be known as Pareto efficiency. This chapter explains that in societies above a certain size, such a peace can only be achieved in a decentralized market system.

Chapter 3 explains that property is a legal concept with three dimensions: the right to enjoy, modify, and transfer the resource you own. Understanding these dimensions of property, also known as property rights, is the key to understanding whether we should allow people to manage their own resources, or whether we should entrust this management to a central authority such as government. Government fails in managing property because true information on the value of property is only revealed in the market and cannot be plucked from theories put forth in the calculating office of a central planning agency. Entrust to government the management of all resources and democracy would be little else than a joust for resources. Without democratic competition to discipline leaders, even the most clear-headed leaders will succumb to corruption. This chapter explains why private property rights protected by rule-of-law succeed, where central control of resources fails to attain Pareto efficiency.

Chapter 4 explains that when you cannot create private property rights, then you must call on the public sector. This is the only justification for government intervention. At all times government must be ready to devolve management of resources to the private sector once technological advances make it feasible for the private sector to create legally defensible accounts surrounding property.

Chapter 5 argues that to fund government intervention we need taxes. These taxes should minimally disrupt Pareto-efficient exchanges. This chapter explains how to create a Pareto-efficient tax system by minimizing the so-called deadweight loss from taxation.

Chapter 6 unites the economics of the four previous chapters with insights from politics and further explorations of the ideas behind Pareto efficiency. It is the most challenging chapter of the book.

Chapter 7 highlights the dangers that our societies face today. The absence of property rights creates a forum in which social calculations get mixed up. The errors may accumulate to such an extent that an economy founders. The solution to creating Pareto efficiency throughout the world lies in migration. Some countries are to a greater or lesser degree Pareto efficiency. If people can move to countries with Pareto efficiency, they will force the regimes they abandon to reform, while at the same time giving force to the Pareto-efficient societies they join. We may never be able to reach the ideal of Pareto's Republic, but we can certainly get close.

Qualifications needed to understand this book

THIS BOOK IS designed for all readers. It will appeal to anyone interested in understanding how a single principle unites economics and politics to create a new science of peace.

PEACE

2

THE THEME OF THIS BOOK is peace, but not the sort you find being discussed at international arms reduction conferences. This book is about the peace that people arrange between themselves, face to face when they confront each other to dispute the control of some resource. Disputes over resources are the main reason for enduring conflict. Sure, someone can become your enemy because he or she simply does not like the way you look. But such conflicts follow no pattern and must be considered part of the inevitable background noise of living, to which we can reconcile ourselves because for every such idiosyncratic hatred you may find someone who likes you equally well. Likes and dislikes of this sort will balance each other out.

What may not balance out are conflicts over resources. A gold mine can incite generations of miners to battle each other. The never-ending conflicts in Africa bear testimony to the tendency of people to persist in conflicts over resources that matter. Africa is a cautionary tale. What should be the richest continent is the poorest. North America is the richest continent but should really be the poorest because it is relatively impoverished in natural resources. What it lacks in these resources it makes up more than a hundredfold in providing its people with a means by which they can convert their personal antagonisms into mutual riches. America and a few select other parts of the world have figured out the principles of what is coming to be understood as the modern science of peace. This science seeks to understand how to convert hostile conflicts into mutually profitable outcomes. The present book is your guide to this emerging science. So let us start at the beginning and have a look at what previous thinkers had to say on the topic.

Transforming aggression into production

THREE THOUSAND YEARS ago, the Hebrew prophet Isaiah foresaw a day when people would "beat their swords into ploughshares, and their spears into pruning hooks: nation shall not lift sword against nation, neither shall they learn war anymore." We do not know how much progress was made towards his vision in the years that followed. We know that several centuries later Virgil, the court poet and chief propagandist for the Roman emperor Augustus, clearly felt that relations between groups of people were taking a bad turn. In his *Georgics* he wrote that war and crime were ravaging the countryside so that "no meet honour hath the plough; the fields, their husbandmen led far away, rot in neglect, and curved pruning-hooks into the sword's stiff blade are fused and forged." Although Virgil seemed to be cribbing from Isaiah, it was not the case. Virgil had no knowledge of Isaiah. A thousand years of history and thousands of miles of sea separated the two. Yet both used the same image to capture the idea that the step between mowing wheat and mowing down an enemy is all too short.

The image of a person beating his or her sword into a ploughshare is powerful because it acknowledges the complexity of human aggression and suggests a means of harnessing it to some peaceful, productive end. The idea of peace as a productively managed conflict arising from the ongoing animosities and tensions between people is not new. Chinese emperors sometimes went to war with the barbarians on their frontiers, but most of the time kept them quiet with bribes. The empire became so skilled at this form of violence management that it eventually absorbed most marauders in a mutually beneficial relationship. In the Middle Ages, European peasants paid armed thugs hefty sums to provide protection against other marauding bandits. It took hundreds of years to work out ever better terms for both sides. Modern democracies that tax their citizens in an orderly manner and spend the money according to public wishes can trace their ancestry to these early attempts to transform violence into something fruitful. One can even find the idea of managed peace in the myth of St. Francis of Assisi who convinced a wolf to stop terrorizing the villagers of Gubbio in return for a regular handout of food, and in the story of Saint Gall who gave bread to a monstrous bear in return for the security of his Swiss parishioners.

In these examples the peaceful solution does not try to eliminate the tensions that give rise to the conflict. Philosophers have noted that the elimination of aggression might even deny us our humanity. Karl Popper wrote in *The Open Society and Its Enemies* that "a human society without conflict would be society not of friends but of ants." The trick instead is to travel from conflict to peace by making both sides see their common interest. Peace is an ongoing process that channels instincts of aggression and acquisitiveness into pursuits which, if they cannot always be called selfless, may at least add to someone's well-being without causing intractable resentments in others.

How to get a peace that transforms aggression into something productive captivates scholars and is the subject of this book. The challenge is to decide whether the transformation of aggression into peace is something we can only grope towards, or whether some formula exists for it. The Pharisaic rabbi Hillel the Elder had such a formula in mind when he stated that "What is hateful to you, do not do to your neighbour: that is the whole Torah, the rest is commentary." This was a very precise mathematical statement of social obligations. It sought perfect balance in every exchange of effort or resources between people. Perfect balance meant you did not take advantage of someone when he or she was down to buy his or her farm at a depressed price. Hillel's balance was a strict and highly specific formula for human interaction.

Rabbi Hillel's rule for balance in social interactions was one of many variants on what has come to be known as the Golden Rule. Plato also believed in a form of the Golden Rule, but in his version, a cadre of exceptionally gifted leaders had to clarify how this rule should be applied. In the 19th century a group calling themselves Utilitarians actually proposed a mathematical formula for peace and prosperity. That formula emerged from the stipulation that societies should work in a way to maximize the sum of happiness of their members. Karl Marx also turned his hand to producing a formula for social peace. He was among the first in history to produce a reasonably consistent argument for why a society should exterminate broad sections of its own population in the interests of prosperity and eventual peace.

Today a science of peace is emerging that tries to unite strands from all of the social sciences to ask how the task of transforming aggression into something of mutual benefit can be accomplished. One sub-branch of this emerging science calls itself "peace economics" and of it Raul Caruso writes

> The core of peace economics has to be found first in the study of the interplay between productive and unproductive activities within societies. This is useful to understand both the long-run determinants of economic prosperity and the shaping and stability of institutions governing economic and societal life. In addition, it also contributes to understand the economic causes and pre-conditions which make actual violent conflicts possible. (page 3)

Peace economics is but one legion in the army now mustering under the banner of the science of peace. Behind the banner stands a concept. It is called the principle of Pareto efficiency, and it can be used to explain how the private economy and the public sector should work individually, and together.

Social accounting

BEFORE JUMPING INTO a discussion of Pareto efficiency we need to understand that no matter what approach to peace one takes, all approaches assume that some balance must exist in relations between people if they are to live in a society. The main contenders in recent history vying for the credit for some formula that captures this balance have been Marxists, Platonists, Utilitarians, Golden Rulers, and other offshoots from these schools of thought. This book will not look deeply into any of these philosophies; it is enough to accept that they shared a belief in the need to balance a type of ledger that one might call the "social accounts." All systems of social accounting, even communism, try to keep a tally of who owes whom what for material property exchanged or favours done.

All groups of people need a social accounting system so that they can coordinate their activities and decide how to use their resources. If your balance is in good standing with me, then you can ask me for help, or the loan of my car. Positive balances give people the means to cooperate with each other and perform collective activities, such as raising a barn or more recently organizing a flash mob. Without a sense of balance in these accounts people either disperse and the group disintegrates, or else people suffer and grow bitter at accumulating injustices. More generally, social accounting is a method for ensuring self-equilibrating exchanges that create balance between what people put into society and what they get out. Without this balance, the links between individual elements of the system threaten to dissolve and the system may lose its coherence.

The most remarkable social dissolution in recent memory took place between 1989 and 1992 when the East Bloc communist countries threw off Marxism in favour of free markets. One favourite slogan among workers just before the fall was "you pretend to pay us and we pretend to work." "What is two hundred meters long and eats cabbage?" asked the Soviet joke. "The queue in front of a butcher's shop," was the answer. Citizens of the East Bloc had a heightened sense of the absurd sharpened through living in a system of economic mismatching where there was little relation between effort and reward, or prices and demand.

Without balance in social accounts, people grew estranged from government and from each other to the point where it was not revolution that brought down the East Bloc, but the dissolution of countless unbound parts.

Two types of social accounting

WHILE THERE IS much disagreement over how to balance the finer points of social accounts, a fairly clear division of opinion about the overall approach has emerged. Some believe that the best way to do so is to use the authority of an all-powerful government; others believe in more personal, face-to-face balancing. The terms you will hear scholars use are vertical (or centralized) coercive control, and horizontal (or decentralized) voluntary control. Both are what you might call information management systems that tally what people contribute and what they take from society. Yet both work very differently from each other.

Under central control, someone in power dictates the use of resources to stifle conflicts between his or her subjects. Dictators are not the only ones who can exert this kind of control; so can village elders or respected community figures who impose their wills by force of custom. The moment an individual resolves disputes coercively or by using tactics of social pressure, he or she becomes an exponent of vertical control. Under lateral control, people must agree between themselves about how resources are to be used. Disagreements can be adjudicated by impartial arbiters of disputes, such as property rights courts. In principle, neither system is to be preferred over the other. Both are adaptations to particular circumstances. If Darwinism has taught us anything it is that adaptations survive only when they are advantageous.

What is the advantage of central control? Societies that use the coercive power of the state or the weight of custom to balance social accounts can spare themselves the bother of investing in the legal apparatus needed to protect property rights. Central control relieves people from haggling over prices or engaging in long legal disputes over private property. That burden all falls to the planners.

There are also disadvantages to central control. The larger the centrally controlled society grows, the more distant rulers become from their subjects. Governments that must decide what clothing people will wear and how to house them have to scrabble for information on their needs and their capacity to contribute. Simply asking people is misleading because talk is cheap. People will exaggerate their needs. This is why during their brief existence during the 20th century, centrally planned economies raised armies of managers and internal spies to sense the popular mood and root out shirkers, and on a more sophisticated plane, applied so-called input-output techniques for representing the entire economy as a spreadsheet capable–in theory–of balancing society's accounts.

Yet even if planners can get the calculation right, and the "if" is big, central control comes burdened with another challenge. It concentrates power and creates the temptation to steal. The manager of a state company can pay his or her workers less than their contribution to production and pocket the difference for his or her own benefit. Poor social accounting due to theft sends the message to workers that it makes little sense to devote energy to the job. On the flip side, consumers become demoralized when they receive shoddy goods, and when they suffer shortages that result from corruption by managers.

A solution to the problem of official corruption is to impose strict rules on those in control. Yet shearing the administrator of discretionary powers atrophies bureaucratic muscles and slows the organizational nerves needed to respond to the changing demands and abilities of the people. Confucian ethics that tried to raise the personal standards of administrators were an attempt to prevent bureaucratic stagnation. The hope was that once cured of their rapacious tendencies by the teachings of Confucius, mandarins could be trusted to use wide discretionary powers in the best interests of the empire. This ethic had some success in containing corruption but produced a conservative mindset ill-suited to dealing with sudden challenges. In communism, the makers of the Russian Revolution tried to instil a similar sense of custodianship coupled with dynamism.

They made enormous strides in certain industries, but an influx of careerists diluted the pool of enthusiasts and eventually produced a cynical bureaucracy whose theft of public property could only be contained by the most stifling rules. As both societies grew and the challenges of balancing social accounts in a central registry mounted, neither imperial China nor communist Russia could find in their administrative systems the key that enabled them to continue their reigns.

Instead of having someone above us keep accounts on our behalf, we might think of balancing these ledgers by ourselves. The reason to consider this is the reason that made central control founder: institutionalized lack of honesty. Perhaps by dealing face-to-face with each other, people can make their true desires known and respected. For this to happen and for individuals to become their own accountants, they must become masters of some little part of their domains. Without control over some resource, they have nothing to balance and decentralized accounting becomes at best a byword for chaos. So, for instance, being able to decide how to use your time allows you to perform favours in return for the promise of favours from others. Being able to call a farm your own allows you to trade its product for processed goods. The fact of owning human and physical resources empowers the individual to make calculations about the worth of his or her property and how it should be used.

Here then is a possible basis for creating a system of social accounts that does not rely on the coercion of central planners. A system of privately owned property puts two powerful forces for honest social accounting into play—precisely the forces that central control lacks. The first force is called competition. It follows from the fact that if I offer you ten dollars an hour for your work, then your ownership of your time means that you are free to accept an alternative offer of eleven dollars. Rival buyers find themselves in a situation where each one goads the other to reveal the true price they are willing to pay for your time or any material resources you own. In this manner competition acts as a mechanism for uncovering the truth about willingness to pay. Revealing willingness to pay is the essence of honest social accounting. Honesty has the practical value that it keeps social accounts in balance. If people reveal what they are willing to pay, then they are sending a signal to suppliers who are equally willing to accept such payment. With both parties agreeing on an exchange, there can be no question that some leave the exchange less enhanced than before. Of course, we may trade the Jacobian chair handed down from an ancestor in the time of Queen Anne, and grumble about it, but the bitterness reflects a situation in life rather than the trade we undertake to improve to some degree a life beset by problems and regrets. This type of all-round improvement of a situation is the ink in which socially balanced accounts are penned.

The second force that private ownership puts into play for the honest balancing of social accounts is protection from corrupt or inefficient governments, a protection that frees people to go about their business without fear of having it disrupted by human predators. Governments, by definition, hold a monopoly on force. A corrupt government is one in which a politician or bureaucrat can divert this force. Instead of using it for the public good, he or she uses force for his or her own private interest. The alderperson who uses the argument of eminent domain to expropriate a farm for the benefit of developers who have promised bribes is violating private control over property in a similar, though less obviously violent manner, as the marauder putting farms to the torch. True private property is protected against such depredations by laws that limit the ability of government representatives to use public powers to steal for private benefit. Theft is one of the clearest means by which to throw social accounts out of balance. Private property, if protected by law, discourages government theft. This is the opposite view of that held by the 19th century French anarchist Pierre Joseph Proudhon who quipped that "property is theft." But a less well known quote of Proudhon's is that "property is freedom." By that he meant that property allows us to seek out our best destinies and that these destinies lie in property protected by the law. The law constrains us, but in so doing frees us to act within limits understood by all. But that is philosophy. This book is about science, the science of peace.

Private property is at the heart of decentralized social accounting because property can be measured. We can better appreciate the importance of property rights as a method of measurement by looking at how people resolve disagreements over matters that have nothing to do with property. Spiritual and emotional issues are among the most contentious we know. One reason for this is that they defy attempts at measurement. They are hard to quantify and so offer little that a science of peace can be built upon. Ultimately, science is about understanding and controlling your environment, and what you cannot measure, you cannot control. John Chipman quotes Nobel Prize winning economist Ragnar Frisch, who summed it up nicely: "The real advances in science begin on the day that it is realized that vague common sense notions must be replaced by notions capable of objective definition" (page 59). A lack of objective definition and measurement is why matters of the heart remain the Wild West of human relations. There is no way to tally in a manner all can accept which side puts more into a romance or a friendship. Without such a tally, no good idea of balance in the relationship can be communicated to outside observers, and so society has no formal ability to dictate a peace of the heart. This is why personal relations are often chaotic and can be contained, if at all, only by religious or social appeals to the conscience. This is why property, which is measurable to some degree, can, with lesser controversy, help balance social accounts.

What does efficiency mean?

WHEN INDIVIDUALS AGREE without coercion about how to use resources, they are approaching a condition that a 19th century railroad engineer who switched into the study of the social sciences at the age of forty-five, identified as having certain desirable features. Vilfredo Pareto, of whom I will say more in the next chapter, defined a particular distribution of resources as being efficient if no one could be made better off by a change in the distribution without making at least one person worse off. If you have an attic full of junk, then a middleman known as a picker can pay you a few dollars and convey the contents of the attic to someone who sees it as treasure. Pickers are emissaries of Pareto because they seek to move resources around in such a way that no one is hurt and at least one person benefits. The picker's job is only done when there are no more deals to be had that satisfy at least one person and harm no one else. This end state of the market, in which all gains from trade are exhausted, is known in economics as Pareto efficiency.

Societies geared toward Pareto efficiency seem to share three key features. First, any process leading to Pareto efficiency limits, but does not completely erase, the downside of agreements over how to use property. Since the agreement is entered into voluntarily, one can believe that both parties will have explored the personal consequences of their decision to shake hands. We can expect no closer an examination of the facts than that made by those most directly concerned. In this sense, Pareto-efficient agreements motivate all parties to think before leaping, and in so doing to avoid leaping into the more obvious pitfalls. Second, a society geared towards Pareto efficiency is one that thwarts the risky ventures of social planners who forget the individual in their pursuit of collectivist visions.

Finally, and perhaps most importantly, Pareto efficiency provides society with a flexible form of social accounting. It does not require that all decisions benefit everyone equally, as in a strictly egalitarian society, but simply that these decisions harm no one. Such flexibility immensely broadens the scope of how property can be used, yet still within humane limits. In addition to their humane qualities, the three features of Pareto efficiency also tend to support economic growth. The evidence overwhelmingly shows that nations with Pareto-efficient dispute resolution mechanisms are among the richest in the world.

The dividend of the peace of Pareto

ECONOMISTS HAVE BEEN at pains to point out that Pareto efficiency is a concept, not a method. What they are getting at is that there are many ways to achieve Pareto efficiency. Nothing says that, in principle, a mad dictator with a cowlick and a jutting jaw cannot get the trains to run on time and provide jobs for all. Alternatively, nothing says that joint-stock companies raising venture capital in exchange for shares cannot convince a multitude of builders, suppliers, and holders of rights-of-way to construct railways of equal or greater precision than the dictator's. Pareto efficiency can be an end state for both the dictator and the corporation, but it is not a road map. The question one must ask is how to get there, if such is our goal. Through centralized and absolute government control, or decentralized decision-making epitomized by a free market in property rights? Do we choose cowlicks and jutting jaws, or opt for top hats and joint-stock ventures?

The answers to these questions are, after many failed social experiments, starting to become conclusive. Consider nations that are so similar in their basic makeup that they could be thought of as twins. In 1953, Korea split in two after a civil war. North Korea came under a tyrant who saw enemies lurking at every turn. He resolved conflict by snatching the nation's property and by abolishing human rights. People could no longer fight over property because it had been removed from their sphere of influence. Since then, generations of North Koreans have toiled in poverty and grown accustomed to famine and living in a climate of government-generated paranoia that distracts the people from the true cause of their woes. They have peace of a sort, but one that comes at a high price. South Korea, meanwhile, converted to a democracy. Its government allowed individuals the freedom to exchange private property under laws that were the same for all. It is now one of the richest countries in the world.

Less extreme, but similar differences can be seen between Pakistan and India. As Pakistan became increasingly authoritarian and arbitrary in its management of the economy during the late 1980s, its economic growth levels dipped and endemic violence began to simmer. At the same time, governments in India were weaning themselves from their addiction to centralized socialist planning of the economy. They tried to create a stable investment climate in which private individuals could determine how they would cultivate their resources. India now has a middle class while Pakistan remains in a condition of economic uncertainty. Haiti and the Dominican Republic share the island of Hispaniola, but they share little else. Haiti jumps from mob rule, to rule by corrupt dictators, and occasionally, to rule by ineffectual elected politicians, and is the poorest nation in the western hemisphere. The Dominican Republic is what the World Bank calls an "upper-middle income developing country" with reasonably secure property rights. Riots and tumult have no place in that country, and the average Dominican earns nearly ten times as much as the average Haitian. The list of twins goes on and includes the former West and East Germanys, and many sub-national jurisdictions.

These casual observations on the value of property rights have formal scientific support. In the late 1980s and early 1990s, under the impetus of economist and Fraser Institute founder Michael Walker, fellow economists Stephen Easton and Walter Block, and Nobel Prize winners Milton Friedman, Gary Becker, and

Douglass North led several weekend retreats to determine how property should be measured and quantified into a single number. The method they worked out is now famously known as the *Index of Economic Freedom*. As they developed the index further, James Gwartney and Robert Lawson found indications that economic freedom and prosperity go hand-in-hand. While there are still many details to work out, these types of study are powerful enough to have attracted a fan club for property rights and to form part of the mission statement of the World Bank, which is "to help people help themselves and their environment by providing resources, sharing knowledge, building capacity, and forging partnerships in the public and private sectors." By helping people to help themselves, the bank is talking as openly as it dare about the benefits of property rights.

Yet we need to keep an open mind. As impressive as the achievements of societies based on property rights are, these rights are not ideals. They are tools. The trick is to recognize which tool is the right one for the job. Under the right conditions, property rights can act as Pareto-efficient "instruments" of peace because they embody a "negotiating rule." A negotiating rule is similar to an accounting procedure. Under Pareto efficiency, disagreements over the use of property must be resolved to the benefit of at least one party and should not harm any other party. Both seek to strike some balance in transactions. Accounts cannot be balanced without some sense of proportion at least, and a method for measuring at best. Property rights provide such rules.

The achievements of societies with secure property rights are impressive, but it is counterproductive to tout property rights as a panacea for creating wealth. Small, stable communities can dispense with elaborate notions of property and rely more on custom and tradition to resolve disputes over resources and balance social accounts. Their approach to dispute resolution is an efficient response to their economic reality. As Harold Demsetz, the pioneer of the study of the evolution of property rights explained in 2002,

> A small isolated village within the boundaries of which residents remain for most of their lives is a setting in which collective decision making becomes practical. The community, in a team effort, can build a bridge over a local creek, and the effort can be enjoyable precisely because it is undertaken collectively. An economizing problem that is localized to a particular family is compact. Generally, the preferred method of resolving it will involve mutual assistance guided by sympathetic feelings, not explicit cash payments linked to third-party-enforced contractual agreements. (page 661)

In contrast to such informal means of resolving differences over how to use resources, sophisticated property rights systems are expensive to create and maintain. They require the protection of impartial courts and honest police, a political system that does not meddle with the courts, a cadre of professional lawyers and the educational infrastructure to train them, and precise instruments to measure and parcel out resources.

If people in a society are going to pay the price for property rights, the reason for doing so must lie in their utility. This utility becomes clear as a society grows and people in it become strangers to each other. Small, stable groups can dispense with formal property rights because they rely on intimacy and empathy to balance social accounts. In a large, fast-moving society these qualities are absent on a scale that encompasses everyone. A forum for exchange such as eBay could not work using informal agreements to pay or assurances that one day the purchaser will find himself in a position to help the seller. Instead, what is necessary to make eBay and other impersonal systems of exchange function in a large anonymous society are formal property rights protected by the law. Such rights are the basis of a flexible social accounting system. The resulting peace is Pareto-efficient, and its dividend is economic prosperity. This is not logically evident, but I will explain it in detail in the pages that follow.

When property rights fail

IF PROPERTY RIGHTS are nothing more than instruments for securing a certain type of peace, then we should maintain and even upgrade those instruments from time to time. This means ensuring that courts are honest, and that we are open to new technological advances in measurement and classification. Advances should allow for the establishment of previously unheard-of types of property rights. Examples are the creation of intellectual property rights, and new methods of measuring and tracking schools of fish by satellite that may one day allow trade to govern their exploitation rather than multi-national pirates who devastate marine life with impunity.

Yet sometimes there is no tool for the job. As the example of international fishing shows, sometimes property rights cannot be created. This is where it may be profitable and wise for government to step in and simulate Pareto efficiency. By recognizing the potential and the limits of private property as a mechanism for peace, we get an idea of the proper extent and role of government intervention in our lives. The dividing line separates the domains of private and public initiative. The line we draw between the two should depend on the costs and benefits of defining and protecting property.

The costs and benefits of creating property rights are the only calculations that guide government's existence in Pareto's Republic. Fairness, social conscience, social justice, and other creeds have a role in the republic, but only as the result of voluntary private initiative. Government, which is the unique instrument of coercion, must use its muscle only to further Pareto efficiency. It may blunder in its quest, but the blunders should not systematically favour one group of people over another. Systematic favouritism sets people against each other in a way that upsets social accounts and ultimately leads not to peace, but to strife.

This seemingly narrow view of government's role is not a prescription for small government *per se*. Government may still distribute money to the poor and build hospitals in Pareto's Republic, provided these activities are what economists call "public goods." This is but one of several paradoxical features of Pareto's Republic. This book explains these paradoxes in the course of explaining the payoffs and costs of living in a Pareto-efficient society. As such, this book is not a biography of Vilfredo Pareto, the man who invented the concept, but an exploration of what might be his most important idea. In learning about what makes Pareto's Republic, this book will take you on a tour of the key concepts of public choice, public finance, game theory, and institutional economics, as well as the foundational ideas of economics and some insights from history and sociology. No prerequisites are needed to understand it except a curiosity about a principle that might one day become humanity's salvation.

PROPERTY   3

I F PEACE IS AN ACCOUNTING problem, who should balance the books? During most of the 20th century it was normal to think that government could take care of the ledger. The First World War saw governments of Western countries expand to manage, if not outright own, vast tracts of their economies. The Great Depression and then the Second World War saw further expansions of government. Crises were the immediate cause of these expansions, but later they gained intellectual legitimacy from Marxist thinkers in Russia, and Keynesians in Europe and North America. As economic stagnation began to afflict Western countries, the question arose as to whether big government, instead of helping the economy, could actually stifle it. The questioning grew more urgent during the collapse of the East Bloc in 1989. A different view of the relative roles of government and the private sector gained impetus partly from these developments, and partly from the award of the Nobel Prize in economics to economists, historians, and political scientists who clarified in a scientific manner the circumstances in which individuals could balance social accounts on their own and those in which government had to step in. As economist Robert Heilbroner wrote in 1992,

> There is today widespread agreement, including among most socialist economists, that whatever form advanced societies may take in the twenty-first century, a market system of some kind will constitute their principal means of coordination. That is a remarkable turnabout from the situation only a generation ago, when the majority of economists believed that the future of economic coordination lay in a diminution of the scope of the market and an increase in some form of centralized planning. (page 75)

The thinkers responsible for this turnabout focused on how property rights, laws, and customs could serve as the medium through which individuals balanced social accounts in a Pareto-efficient manner. The point at which much of this reflection started was Pareto himself.

Enter Pareto

EVERY MOVEMENT NEEDS some kind of an apostle to give it a human face. A candidate for the apostle of this peace movement is an Italian railroad engineer who at the age of forty-five turned his interest to the social sciences where, according to Nobel Prize winning economist Henry Schultz, his range of interest embraced "… not only economics, but also sociology, history, mathematics, and other fields." Among the founders of economics Pareto was not unique in the breadth of his interests or the seeming incongruity of his profession. John Stuart Mill was a civil servant for the East India Company and later a Member of Parliament. David Ricardo, the founder of trade theory, was a stock broker and also entered Parliament. Thomas Malthus began as an Anglican country curate, while Karl Marx alternated between journalism and political agitation, and William Stanley Jevons did an extended tour in Australia testing the quality of coinage for the mint. Schultz explains that those who read Pareto's original writings

> will be repaid a thousand fold, for they will then discover how incomplete and misleading is the discussion in most current texts of such fundamental subjects as utility, demand, marginal productivity, and maximum satisfaction, as compared with Pareto's treatment of the same subjects. They will, in short, learn how classical economic theory has, chiefly through the labors of Walras and Pareto, been unified, amended, completed and surpassed. (page 740)

Schultz was writing in 1928 at a time when economists were just beginning to discover Pareto, and since then, Pareto's reputation has continued its steady rise.

Pareto might have been mortified to be called an apostle of anything, but might also have understood how the term might apply to him figuratively. What he might not have understood was the subsequent far-reaching application of a concept he developed in 1902 to settle an academic spat over the merits of free trade. In this debate with a young mathematician named Gaetano Scorza, Pareto was forced to come up with a definition of economic efficiency. For Pareto, an exchange of goods between two people was "improving" if it left at least one of the parties to the exchange better off and no one in society worse off. An exchange could go further and become Pareto-efficient if all parties concerned had exhausted all the potential "gains from trade." Today, a Pareto-efficient exchange is taken to be the type of deal that once done, cannot be renegotiated in any way that would make one person better off without making at least one other worse off. Pareto-efficient exchanges squeeze the maximum out of what people can each profitably gain from agreeing to an exchange.

According to John Chipman, Pareto's chief intellectual biographer and himself a prominent mathematical economist, the debate with Scorza on economic efficiency passed into obscurity, as most such arguments do. It was not until the 1920s that economists rediscovered the principle of efficiency that Pareto developed in 1902, and not until 1950 that it became widely acknowledged that Pareto was its originator, and while Pareto's insight has spurred much new research, it is only now starting to become a part of the vocabulary of non-specialists. Perhaps economists are to blame for not advertising to a broader public what is one of the foundational ideas of their profession. The reason to market this idea is that it offers to the public several things everyone values: a sense of community, security, and even prosperity. A concept capable of doing this is worthy of attention.

The three pillars of Pareto efficiency

THE FRENCH PHILOSOPHER Pascal said that to understand a whole we need to start by understanding the parts. Pareto efficiency as a total concept is linked to prosperity, but before we can see why that is so, we need to examine what might be called the three pillars of Pareto efficiency. It is upon these pillars that prosperity rests.

The first pillar of Pareto efficiency is social mindedness. Societies geared towards generating Pareto efficiency have a strong impetus to short-circuit the conflict between individual and collective well-being. This is one of the first lessons we are taught as children. Do not butt ahead of others in line; do not leave a mess behind you. Children learn many such lessons in the long course of their socialization. The basis of the lessons is that the ego cannot expand without limit and that our limits are determined in part by the presence of others. Pareto efficiency embodies this basic childhood lesson explicitly. In a Pareto-efficient society, discussions about how to use resources tend to explore outcomes that benefit at least one, and perhaps all parties to the discussion, without hurting anyone. Pareto efficiency asks that the most extreme form of democracy underlie all decisions about property. A project must get a 100 percent vote of approval by all parties concerned, or the deal is off. Researchers working in the budding field of neuroeconomics, such as Paul Zak, believe that growing up in Pareto-efficient systems may not only moderate behaviour but may also shape the individual, enhancing his or her concern for others, thereby further enhancing Pareto efficiency, in a continuing "virtuous circle." He writes that

> Market exchange itself may lead to a society where individuals have stronger character values. The clearest evidence for this are the studies of fairness in small-scale societies conducted by Heinrich and his colleagues. They showed that the likelihood of making fair offers to a stranger in one's society is more strongly predicted by the extent of trade in markets than any other factor they have found. Exchange is inherently other-regarding—both you and I must benefit if exchange is to occur. In this sense, exchange in markets is virtuous; one must consider not only one's own needs but also the needs of another. (page xv)

The second pillar of Pareto efficiency is insurance against governments or any potentially rapacious force that would sacrifice some for the good of others. To understand this idea, take the opposite example of Marxists and their milder cousins, the socialists. Marxists were comfortable eliminating dominant economic classes for "the greater good." Socialists accepted that the rich could be made to suffer in order to help the poor and that the rights of individuals could be trampled in order to favour certain groups, as is the case in the closed-shop union, where workers are forced to join the union and obey its rules in order to obtain employment. Marxist regimes, and to a lesser degree socialist systems of the mid-20th century, made no apology for their concentration camps, mass sterilizations, one-child policies, and family-wrecking expropriations of farms, all done in the name of "the people." Decisions about human gain and loss were the stated business of such regimes. Today's more benign versions of these movements have dialed down the rhetoric of violence but still accept a calculus that trades the well-being of some against that of others.

While such regimes may sometimes produce remarkable accomplishments in architecture, military prowess, and education, their leaders can use extreme means to achieve their ends. They have ignored the 100 percent approval characteristic of Pareto efficiency. This characteristic, the second pillar of Pareto efficiency, is a fail-safe mechanism that limits the adverse effects of decisions about how to use physical and human resources. The second pillar arises from the fact that Pareto efficiency does not admit that the well-being of one person should be sacrificed for that of another.

The third pillar of Pareto efficiency is that it provides a flexible system of social accounting that does not require that everyone get an equal benefit out of an exchange. All that Pareto efficiency requires is that, at the very least, one person profit and none is harmed. This is perhaps the most remarkable and subtle aspect of Pareto efficiency. To see why, we need once again to look at an opposite case. In small groups living in stable communities, Pareto efficiency is of little interest or importance. Their members live in fixed relation to each other, which allows them to go beyond efficiency to attain fairness. More specifically, the community's intimate nature allows it to identify and correct imbalances caused by those who are considered too greedy or too lucky in their affairs. Community members may depend upon each other to such a degree in order to survive that the idea of an explicit exchange of goods may not even arise. Such is the case in an Israeli kibbutz, a Mennonite community, or among the Bushmen of the Kalahari. The main challenges in their lives are collective. Collective challenges inculcate an egalitarian mindset.

These societies usually rely on some idea of reciprocity. Scholars call such notions of reciprocity Golden Rules. Those rules aim for everyone to contribute fairly to communal work. The problem with Golden Rules is that as a community grows and people become distant from one another, it becomes difficult to enforce a uniform notion of fairness in exchange. When a society grows into a collection of fast-moving, anonymous individuals, a more flexible and quantifiable version of the Golden Rule is necessary. That version is Pareto efficiency. It does not require that the fruits of an exchange be equally divided between both parties. An exchange is efficient if it makes at least one party better off and none worse off. The balance may not be perfect as it might seem to be in Golden Rule communities, but it is sufficiently satisfactory, even for perfect strangers. These types of exchanges need to be facilitated so that a society can continue to grow.

A sense of community, stability, and a certain flexibility in the exchanges we can make with others sound fine, but how does any of this lead to prosperity? To answer this we need to know what prosperity is. The concept has a static and a dynamic aspect. Imagine you inherit a farm with rich land, equipment, and livestock. That is prosperity of a static sort. Finding new ways to use your land to maximize its value can lead to prosperity of a dynamic sort. Paul Romer, possibly the leading expert in the study of economic growth, illustrated this point by noting that

> In most coffee shops, you can now use the same size lid for small, medium, and large cups of coffee. That was not true as recently as 1995. That small change in the geometry of the cups means that a coffee shop can

serve customers at lower cost. Store owners need to manage the inventory for only one type of lid. Employees can replenish supplies more quickly throughout the day. Customers can get their coffee just a bit faster. Although big discoveries such as the transistor, antibiotics, and the electric motor attract most of the attention, it takes millions of little discoveries like the new design for the cup and lid to double a nation's average income.

The search to enhance the use of resources is not exclusive to societies geared towards Pareto efficiency, yet such societies are particularly successful in this search because of the way they allow people to express talent. Pareto-efficient societies encourage the use of talents that can benefit their owners and others, but harm no one else. Societies that allow deviations from Pareto efficiency allow darker talents to be expressed, such as a knack for preying on the riches of others or simply indulging in a taste for mayhem. Economists Kevin Murphy, Andrei Shleifer, and Robert Vishny expanded on the differences between Pareto-efficient and predatory societies in a 1991 article by observing that which activities the most talented people choose can have significant effects on the allocation of resources.

> When talented people become entrepreneurs, they improve the technology in the line of business they pursue, and as a result, productivity and income grow. In contrast, when they become rent seekers, most of their private returns come from redistribution of wealth from others and not from wealth creation. As a result, talented people do not improve technological opportunities, and the economy stagnates. (page 505)

As examples of rent-seeking—the act of cutting up society's resources rather than finding better ways to exploit them—they point to Mandarin China, medieval Europe, and African countries in this century where "government service, with the attendant ability to solicit bribes and dispose of tax revenue for the benefit of one's family and friends, was the principal career for the ablest people in the society."

Pareto efficiency as a dynamic concept

PARETO EFFICIENCY IS a broad principle upon which to organize society, but it is not a complete principle. It is mainly useful as a guide to organizing society *once resources have been divided up*. Before such a division, Pareto efficiency is no guide to using resources. This may seem an extremely unlikely nuance to worry about, but it does arise during rare instances of social upheaval and it has some importance in discussions about fairness, as we shall see in the next chapter.

The challenge of coming up with an initial allocation of resources is remote to Western minds, but it was the sort of problem East Bloc countries faced starting in 1989 when they moved from state to private ownership. Pareto efficiency was of little help as a guide to allocating these resources. Think of a society in which the only product one can consume is apples and that government has control over all of them, but wishes to allocate them to its subjects. It can split the apples evenly among citizens, it can give all to one individual and none to others, or it can devise many other splits or "allocations." Any one of these possible allocations is Pareto-efficient! That is because once the split is made, there is no way to intervene and split up the apples again without harming at least one person. Clearly, in a case such as this, Pareto efficiency is no guide for government action.

Some other principle, such as fairness, or even fear, is needed to decide the initial split of resources. In the East Bloc fear was the main motivation for a too quick division of communist property. Journalists have called this restitution "the theft of the century," but East Bloc economists such as Vaclav Klaus and Yegor Gaidar pushed their governments to privatize quickly out of a concern that communism might return should the state be allowed to keep its assets. In addition to seeking to thwart a return to communism, economists sought a restitution of property—fair or not—in part because they believed in something called the "second fundamental theorem of welfare economics."

The second welfare theorem states that if you can distribute to people initial allocations of resources in the form of "lump-sum transfers," that is, without any strings attached, this allocation will, through free trade, lead to a specific Pareto-efficient final distribution of resources. What this means is that if a person is not completely satisfied with the fresh-start package received from government, he or she can seek out other people who have their own packages and trade with them if a mutually agreeable exchange is possible. As Robert Blaug notes, Starr's 1997 explanation of the importance of the second welfare theorem deserves to be cited. Starr writes that the second theorem

> is the basis of the common prescription on public finance that any attainable distribution of welfare can be achieved using the market mechanism and lump-sum taxes (corresponding to the redistribution of endowments). On this basis, public authority intervention in the market through direct

provision of services (housing, education, medical care, child care, etc.) is an unnecessary escape from market allocation mechanisms with their efficiency properties. Public authority redistribution of income should be sufficient to achieve the desired reallocation of welfare while retaining the market discipline for efficient resource allocation. (page 198)

One might think of the second welfare theorem as an adult way of describing what happened to the lunches our parents sent with us to school. There was perhaps nothing fair about who got what in the first round, and if the principal had forced some children to trade their lunches with others, there would have been no guarantee that no child would have been disappointed. Yet somehow, in the schoolyard, pastries, sausages, curries, and even vegetables changed hands until children had undone whatever nutritional or devotional scheme their parents had devised, and the happiness of all had been enhanced. The continued trading that starts to take place after the initial allocation, whether in the schoolyard or the boardroom, leads to a dynamic form of Pareto efficiency, which as we shall now see, is a powerful principle on which to order society.

Property rights and Pareto efficiency

PARETO EFFICIENCY DOES not come about by itself. It needs some sort of medium through which to work. There are two candidates for the job. One is an all-knowing government that resolves differences over the use of resources by drawing up detailed plans for the economy. The other candidate is the individual, empowered to make personal decisions on the use of resources within his or her control. This sphere of control is called private property. Let us start by looking at this second means of attaining Pareto efficiency.

Before we understand how Pareto efficiency and property are linked, we need to ask what is property. This is a question that has been debated before courts over hundreds of years. The lesson from this debate is that there is little practical meaning in simply saying that property belongs to someone. Think of a time-share condominium in Florida. In what sense does a person "own" this property? He or she can perhaps stay there two weeks in the year, and may not modify the interior or allow pets inside. The time-share example illustrates that one should not think simply about owning property, but rather about owning varied claims on resources. The fundamental, but not exhaustive list of claims on resources are the right to use and enjoy the resource, the right to its fruits (such as revenues from the sale of minerals or agricultural output), and the right to modify, sell, or dispose of it as he or she sees fit. The set of these claims are usually called property rights.

Talking of property rights as varying claims to the fruits, use, and disposal of resources may seem contrived, but the degree to which we can understand and appreciate the peace of Pareto depends on how well we can separate the physical image of property from its abstract representation in law. Imagine you own a run-down property from which a non-functioning telephone cable runs into the neighbour's garden, under his house, and out into the street where it connects with the city telephone network. You want to tear the cable out because it is an unsightly coil. Your lawyer sees something different. To him it represents a right-of-way, which would allow you to pass updated telecommunications cables across the property of potentially hostile owners so that you might profitably hook your house up to the city infrastructure. What you see as the physical essence of the wire your lawyer sees as a legal concept.

In a system of property rights Pareto efficiency comes about by trade. If you farm apples and someone else farms oranges, both of you can profit by exchanging some of your product because no one wants to eat only apples or only oranges. Of course some other farmer who produces apples but who adores oranges far more than you may outbid you. His or her greater bid will be the final step towards Pareto efficiency if no one else is willing to offer the orange farmer a similar or even greater bid. In such a case, no one's well-being can be improved without diminishing the well-being of someone else.

Economists call this Pareto efficiency in consumption. If you have inherited a rental property but have no idea of how to run it, you might go bankrupt. You could avoid that fate by selling the property to someone who knows the rental trade. The exchange makes you richer and allows someone with greater expertise to provide others with an enhanced rental service. Then if a major real-estate management firm with even greater skills comes along, it may offer the person who bought your property even more money for it. When property rights end up in the hands of the most efficient manager, economists say that Pareto efficiency in production has been achieved. In the case of both farmers and property managers, Pareto efficiency comes about by exchanging property until it is either in the hands of the ablest managers, or is being consumed by those who are willing to pay the most for it.

The most common objection to this view of Pareto efficiency is that it is incomplete because it does not take into account the manner in which price changes can hurt people. If I run a laundry business, I will not appreciate the arrival of immigrants who are willing to work longer than I am, or have greater skills that allow them to undercut my prices. If I live in a sleepy town and have been considering the purchase of a house, I will not be pleased to see property prices being bid up by rich newcomers from the big city.

By upsetting the market value of property rights, do not these price changes violate Pareto efficiency? Could not the solution to this problem be to create a fourth dimension to property rights? As we've seen, the first three dimensions are the right to enjoy, enhance, and transfer property. How about the right to a guaranteed price for one's property?

This suggestion is by no means far-fetched. Almost every country has some products for which the government tries to fix or set some limit to the price. In developed countries farmers have successfully lobbied governments for "supply management" systems that stop new competitors from entering the industry and driving down the price of agricultural products. In developing countries that balance of power tilts towards city dwellers who manage through government to extract from farmers food at prices below what they would get if they were allowed to sell the good freely.

In some cases this "price-security property right" is formally entrenched in law. Broadcast licenses for cable TV are legally recognized property rights that block entry into the market of other cable companies. The same is true of taxi licenses, milk production quotas, and in a more obscure but no less effective way various trade protection societies such as those run by physicians, chiropractors, plumbers, and lawyers who have organized into official bodies with the legal right to limit entry into their professions by competitors who would drive down the price of their services.

The effect of adding a fourth dimension that guarantees the value of property rights is to violate, or at least diminish, the other three dimensions. A production quota that allows only its holders to sell milk violates the right of cow-owners without a quota to transfer their product to others. Remember that transferability is one of the other three dimensions. Rent control prevents property owners from temporarily transferring their rental property to those willing to pay the most, with the collateral effect of discouraging owners from investing in the upkeep of their rental units. A fixed limit on the number of physicians to be licensed prevents potential physicians from offering their services to potential patients. In these and hundreds of other cases, "price-security property rights" clash with the function of enjoyment, enhancement, and transfer of one's resources.

Whether or not to add this fourth dimension in Pareto's Republic is an extremely complex question, but one that has a clear answer: no. The question is complex because it forces us to understand the difference between initial allocations of resources and continued reallocations based on chance events.

Following an initial allocation of resources economists have shown through the second theorem of welfare economics that there are no price changes because everyone has exploited the situation to the maximum and all profitable trades have been done. The moment resources are allocated only one final set of prices emerges from the haggling that follows in the market. A popular television program illustrates this to perfection. Highly irritated men and women bid for the contents of abandoned storage lockers. Here is the initial allocation. The program follows their attempts then to price, with the help of experts, some musty manuscript or creaky turntable extracted from the miscellany in the locker. This expert price is supposed to be final and in this sense represents the price at which no one is willing to further buy or sell. Once you put resources into peoples' hands, they immediately search out the best use for them and do so Pareto-efficiently because property rights do not allow one to enter into an exchange that harms the other party.

Then chance intervenes. Someone discovers a machine that can clean laundry at a tenth of the previous price. That means my laundry business will suffer due to the competitor who invented the machine. Yes, Pareto efficiency is violated, but it is the workings of chance that have made it so.

To repair or exploit the new opportunities that chance presents, people then once more set about trading resources to find the new Pareto-efficient way of using them. If we were to insulate ourselves from the effects of chance by blocking new inventions then certainly some businesses would continue to survive and some jobs would be preserved, but as the years passed and new discoveries continued to accumulate, a growing pot of gold would be sitting at society's periphery, untouched. Similarly, we could force people to sell food at a fixed low price to areas afflicted by shortages, but the effect would be to discourage the production of food. Who wants to sell anything at less than what it can profitably produce? Fixing prices creates an imbalance in social accounts that eventually leads to shortages and disaster.

What these examples suggest is that there is no way to insulate ourselves from the violations of Pareto efficiency that result from chance. The examples also show that if we stick to protecting the first three dimensions of property rights, namely the rights to enjoy, cultivate, and especially transfer, then we can repair the upsets of adverse, unforeseen events and exploit the possibilities of chance inspirations and discoveries.

The importance of transferability

IT IS DIFFICULT to say which of the three dimensions of property are most important but we can affirm that the right of transfer is of primary importance to Pareto efficiency because it is by reshuffling the ownership of resources that they end up in the most productive hands. To better grasp these ideas, let us take a brief tour of the evolution of property rights over the past several hundred years. The story begins around three hundred years ago, in a period historian Julian Ruff calls "Early Modern Europe."

Early Modern Europe was plagued by arbitrary acts of violence and exploitation, but was also characterized by a broad and systematic attempt by governments to end lawlessness, largely for economic reasons. Acts of casual and random violence were so commonplace as to be hardly noticed. It was a time in which family honour was paramount. Without property to act as dependable collateral, honour was the best guarantee that a family would respect the terms of agreements with other families. Members who debased this ephemeral form of collateral, perhaps by marrying against family wishes, found themselves subject to internecine beatings and even "honour killings." It was also a time when the idea of the individual, someone who could operate fruitfully outside the strictures of group censure, was not widely accepted. Groups protected their members, but any who strayed became prey to the depredations of other clans or gangs. In these environments simmering with conflict, the willingness of employers to invest in training an employee who the next week might be maimed in a brawl was limited, as was the willingness to invest in a factory that might be expropriated by corrupt officials, or "taxed" by organized crime. As Thomas Hobbes who lived at that time wrote in Chapter XIII of *Leviathan*:

> In such condition there is no place for industry, because the fruit thereof is uncertain: and consequently no culture of the earth; no navigation, nor use of the commodities that may be imported by sea; no commodious building; no instruments of moving and removing such things as require much force; no knowledge of the face of the earth; no account of

time; no arts; no letters; no society; and which is worst of all, continual fear, and danger of violent death; and the life of man: solitary, poor, nasty, brutish, and short.

At the start of the Early Modern period some governments began to master the administrative skills necessary to curb arbitrary theft and the violation of human rights. By monopolizing violence and regularizing its application in the form of laws applied equally to all, government was starting to provide a service that is known today as the rule of law. The rule of law does not mean that courts make perfect judgments, but that the judgments do not arbitrarily favour one group or individual. This even application of law to resources is what began to give property rights their ability to balance social accounts in a Pareto-efficient manner. Under rule of law I can protect my property from being expropriated by individuals with a strong aptitude for violence and a lack of moral sense. The only way to make me part with my property is by convincing me peacefully to do so, through the offer of some acceptable form of compensation.

This new protection from the arbitrary application of force allowed property to be transferred between individuals in way that it could find its most productive owner. The prosperity that came with this new flexibility was the peace dividend that resulted from moving closer to life in Pareto's Republic.

The movement towards Pareto's Republic was progressive, depending on a web of positive feedback relations that in non-technical language people call a "virtuous circle." Once the rule of law was established, entrepreneurs were emboldened to invest in machines and factories. These investments in physical "capital" meant that workers could accomplish more than before. One person operating a stamping machine could do the work of thirty blacksmiths pounding on anvils. Increasingly productive workers became increasingly precious to their employers and to the tax-hungry state. As ordinary folk grew in commercial value, states rapidly began to form police forces to protect them, and to hear complaints of violence against them in the courts. The move away from being an expert in personal violence, to becoming an expert in productive activities, enhanced the "productive human capital" of workers. Better trained workers in turn increased the productivity of physical capital. The increased productivity of capital encouraged states to further invest in defining human rights, and so on, within an expanding spiral of prosperity in which sensitive and talented people could separate themselves from the world of violence. Not only could they separate themselves from violence, but these people could also distance themselves from narrow social groups on which they had previously depended for protection. Freed from the pressure to conform, some people could express a range of creativity not possible in settings that had subjected the individual to strict conformity for reasons of group protection.

Countries such as Britain, France, and the Netherlands, which managed to understand the link between property rights (especially their transferability), peace, and even prosperity, saw their economies grow and their tax revenues explode. They came to a new and gentler understanding of how to manage their subjects than in the past. Countries such as Spain and Portugal, who at that time got most of their money from plundering the treasures and riches of South America, remained politically and economically backward. Faraway Peruvian gold shone too brightly for Spanish emperors to notice that the industrial revolutions taking place on their borders went hand-in-hand with political revolutions. Spain limped into the 20th century almost as economically underdeveloped as it had been four hundred years before, caring little for the fate of its mainly illiterate people. Other countries in the 20th century that relied heavily on price controls, such as Argentina and Greece, also underwent protracted periods of stagnation.

It is no accident that the notion of individual rights originated, or at least took flight, in the philosophical talking shops and salons of countries that began reaping the wealth dividend of the peace of Pareto. Philosophy and economic development reinforced each other to lay the basis for what today we consider to be human rights. Under the protection of the state, people were able to concentrate their efforts on educating and training themselves in manufacturing and science, rather than spending hours planning vendettas and mastering combat skills.

It is doubtful, though, whether such rights would have continued to evolve had they not brought prosperity in their wake. This "instrumental" value of human and property rights explains the vehemence with which Karl Marx detested them. As economic philosopher Allen Buchanan notes in his landmark study, *Ethics, Efficiency, and the Market*, Marx saw the basic civil and political legal rights that individuals enjoy in a capitalist system as being valuable "*only* as ways of coping with those sorts of conflicts of interest that are themselves artifacts of the capitalist system" (page 48). To Marx, liberty was simply a necessary evil for coping with capitalist exploitation. Communism he wanted to prove, would reduce scarcity, selfishness, and class divisions to a degree that rights were no longer needed.

I agree with Marx to an extent on this last point; throughout this book I argue that where people can get along without property rights in a way that balances social accounts in a manner acceptable to all, they should do so. The problem, though, is that such outcomes are only possible in small, close-knit societies. In large, fast-moving societies, it becomes impractical to implement the Marxian vision of a society without formal human and property rights, as the following section explains.

Government planning and Pareto efficiency

THE ALTERNATIVE TO reaching Pareto efficiency through property rights is to entrust government with the management of resources. While we might believe that having great confidence in government's abilities as a manager is an out-moded way of thinking, during the 20th century it held pride of place.

So powerful was the belief at that time in central government planning that it gave rise to what was perhaps the most startling phenomenon of the 20th century: mass forced communes. Russia, China, and their smaller imitators tried with varying degrees of success to do away with the money economy and its sub-strate, private property. Communist leaders argued that property was an unjust mechanism on which to base the organization of society. To fill the organizational vacuum created by the disappearance of private property, Soviet ideologists proposed control by a central authority. It was an idea that went far beyond anything Marx had been able to imagine in the mid-19th century.

The problem that vexed Soviet technocrats was that, unlike a small voluntary commune such as a kibbutz or a hippie farm where members share the same ideals, the Soviet Union was a vast commune imposed on what is perhaps the most diverse group of peoples in the world. The Soviet approach to the coordination problem had two thrusts: altering the mind and eliminating enemies of the state. To these ends, the state spent prodigiously on propaganda and gulags. The systematic brainwashing and abuse of human rights that ensued was not the by-product of having a mustachioed sociopath in power, what the Italians called *il baffone*, but was a well-reasoned means, and perhaps the only means, of determining how resources were going be used in the absence of private property rights.

Soviet planners had to resort to crude social engineering to create some balance between needs and means because they lacked essential information. The lack of information about the human resources available to the regime was particularly acute. This was partly because people hid their true talents for fear of being exploited by factory bosses. If you felt you had a few more hours of work left in you at week's end, this was the last thing you wanted to show. Your boss would push you to produce more for little or no extra pay and claim for him or herself the bragging rights for increased factory production. It was wiser to hide your personal "excess capacity" and divert it to working in your garden, or fixing your car, or simply getting drunk. In an economy where the individual is the master of his or her own time and can use it with the full protection of the law, the opposite is true. In free market economies people boast of their abilities, and these boasts are put to an immediate test in the workplace. In the Soviet system, you kept your mouth shut for your own good. Today, migrants from the Soviet to a free market system learn, with some resistance, that one must market oneself, and that trumpeting one's qualifications puts one in no danger of being exploited.

Soviet planners should be seen in retrospect as middlemen who acted as the liaison between workers and consumers. As such, they must be considered as arbiters who tried to balance social accounts. One may well ask why these arbiters did not give workers a fair reward. What stopped planners from encouraging workers with the necessary salary increases so that they would meet the needs of consumers? To act as bridges between workers and consumers, central planners needed accurate information, not just on the abilities of workers, but on what consumers were willing to give up, or pay, to satisfy their needs. We have seen that workers had reason to keep their mouths shut, thereby depriving planners of information on productive potential. Consumers, in contrast, had good reason to be vocal in their demands. In an economy based on private property rights, people reveal their wants by putting their money where their mouths are. The more you want of something, the more you will pay to have it. In a socialist economy, people cannot prove the intensity of their desires by showing their willingness to trade their private property, because there is no private property. All that a socialist government has to go on in deciding how to allocate resources is what people tell it, either through the political process, or through agitation and terrorism. People will inevitably exaggerate their needs. Even the most honest socialist planner was caught between the lies that workers told and the lies that consumers told, and had a very tough job balancing the social accounts.

Yet the corruption of social accounts did not end there. Without the restraint of rules, and in the absence of credible signals from consumers and producers, socialist planners succumbed to further devastating compulsions. Either they planned the economy according to their ideological leanings, or simply used their absolute power to rob both workers and consumers. The endemic corruption that corroded the structure of socialist societies could not be stopped. The reason lay in the very logic of central planning. Socialist systems cannot cure corruption by instituting the rule of law because such systems are inherently lawless. Every rule the central planner writes to protect citizens from the arbitrary acts of those in power also strips the planner of a part of his or her ability to manipulate resources. That is because rules necessarily place part of those resources either under the control of the private individual or, at the very least, out of the control of the planner. The moment you protect me from eviction, or arbitrary search, or from having to leave my family to work in a mine, you give me some say, or at least a guarantee, over my physical and personal resources. In so doing, you gradually build for me something resembling property rights. This is why pure central planning depends on the absence of rules.

The absence of rules corrupts socialist planners and makes nonsense of their aim of balancing social accounts. "Socialism with a human face," a phrase Alexander Dubček used during the Prague Spring of 1968, takes on a sinister meaning when the socialism in question relies on coercion. The face may be human, but it is the face of Ozymandias, the despot from Shelley's eponymous poem, with its "frown, and wrinkled lips, and sneer of cold command."

The challenge of incorrect information

THE TALE OF communist mismanagement is troubling, but it does not prove that central planning is necessarily inferior to decentralized decision making. Systems with and without property rights both face informational challenges in balancing social accounts. The sophisticated socialist thinker Oscar Lange stated that provided a centrally planned government knew all the needs and abilities of its citizens, what economists more formally call the equations of demand and supply, it could allocate resources in such a way as to mimic Pareto efficiency.

In the next installment of what came to be known as the socialist calculation debate, Nobel Prize winning economist Friedrich Hayek argued that central planners could never collect information on the abilities and needs of their people because such information is only revealed through the private deal-making that takes place between people in settings such as markets.

Only the private individual has the "knowledge of particular circumstances of time and place" and he or she will only reveal these in a gradual process of determining from others what is available and what their needs are. I know I need a bicycle to get to work, so I search among sellers for the best deal. My view on the worth of bicycles is set against that of others; the final price of bicycles that results from our demands upon producers is a public advertisement leading everyone interested to consider whether his or her willingness to pay exceeds that of others. During this process individuals specialize in collecting the sort of data that concerns them specifically. Hayek's insight was that central planners simply cannot collect such information because it can only emerge from a process of individuals exchanging property rights. In this vein a central planner sitting in a remote office, solving hundreds of equations of demand and supply to arrive at a final list of who should produce what and who could consume it was an act of pretension, even self-delusion, mainly because the data for such an exercise could never be collected in a centrally planned economy.

In Hayek's view, the proof is not in devising a recipe for the pudding, but in the making of it. What Hayek did not add, but which would fit perfectly into his way of thinking, was that even if central planners did have access to all the information possible, they would likely abuse it because of their monopoly control over coercion. Abuse can take many shapes. Managers may simply ignore information about consumer needs and working conditions. Or they might barter for their own private advantage factory materials that do not belong to them. Human trafficking is amongst the most troubling of abuses of centrally controlled systems. Generals may force their soldiers to labour on their country homes, or rent out this labour on the black market. A look at the enormous problems that private companies have in controlling the abuse of inside information by employees who want to quickly enrich themselves on the stock market gives only a small hint of how great the abuse of information can be in a centrally managed economy. At least in a private economy, firms that abuse inside information see their stocks plummet and eventually disappear from the market. A centrally planned economy where managers abuse the information they control cannot disappear the way a private firm can.

The high cost of property rights

SOCIETIES BASED ON Pareto efficiency and the property rights that support it enjoy significant benefits. Yet one should hesitate to advise property rights as the path to Pareto efficiency in all circumstances, in the same way that one would hesitate to advise all to drive a Bugatti. Property rights, like Bugattis, do not come free. The technology needed to measure property, the brain and muscle needed to rule over it in courts and from patrol cars, and the resources needed to ensure that the public custodians of property rights are behaving honestly, all cost society a small fortune.

In a celebrated article entitled *Toward a Theory of Property Rights,* Harold Demsetz argued that property rights come about as the result of cost-benefit calculations. Serfdom in Europe was once a form of slavery from which there was no escape. This was a constricting situation for both sides because the serf might have been more productive working as a merchant in a large town. However, the serf was not able to cut a deal with the lord because there were no courts or police that could guarantee that the former serf would pay his debt to the lord after moving away and starting his new profession. Eventually laws and an enforcement apparatus evolved that allowed serfs to buy their freedom by credibly promising their lords payments out of their future free wages.

The evolution of laws and enforcement was the force that drove down the cost of establishing the human property rights over which serfs and lords could bargain. Demsetz provided other historical examples to support his contention that the costs of creating property rights need to be compared to the benefits they generate before a verdict can be reached about relying on them. His conclusion was that once the results on performance are in, we may find that property rights are not the best way to resolve every conflict over the use of resources.

Demsetz's work followed on from insights by a young economist plying his trade in London in the 1930s. Nobel Prize winning economist Ronald Coase demonstrated in a 1937 article entitled *The Nature of the Firm* that firms balance the benefits of property rights against their costs. Corporations do not rely on decentralized bargaining over property rights among their employees to get things done, but rather on vertical lines of command and cooperation. Bosses give broad indications of how the corporation's resources are to be used and office workers fill in the gaps by cooperating with each other. Corporations work this way because it is not efficient for every exchange between people to be done for money.

Think of how long it would take to build a skyscraper if all workers were independent bargainers who had to write individual contracts with all other workers. Who can borrow Martin's arc welder and at what price, and how much shall we all pay for the administrative services of Drusilla, would be two of the hundreds of thousands of contracts that would have to be written. It is far more effective for workers and administrators to band together in a firm where the only contracts are the salary paid for a job well done, and the fee charged the customer. These contracts are convenient shorthand for resolving the multitude of conflicts that go into any sort of grand collective enterprise. Even though they appear as flagships of the capitalist system of money and trade, below decks corporations strive to be sharing communities. In a sense, the corporation is a return to an earlier social condition in which the Golden Rule of exact reciprocity applied and in which the costly instrument of property rights was not needed to resolve disputes.

Enter government

IN THE CASE of society, just as in the case of firms, sometimes property rights are too costly to pay for and a hierarchical solution to conflicts is required. Consider a coal-powered electricity plant that spews sulphur into the air. The plant and its customers are happy to do business, but they are violating Pareto efficiency by producing acid rain, which destroys gardens and private forests and thereby violates other people's claims to their own property. It may be too costly for the victims to prove the damage that is being done to them and seek court-ordained compensation. In other words, defining and enforcing property rights to clean air may be impossible. Some economists call this situation "market failure." In the next chapter I explain why market failure is exclusively a failure to define property rights and how this is the only reason in Pareto's Republic for government action.

SPENDING 4

I**N THE EARLY TWENTIETH CENTURY**, economists started thinking about Pareto efficiency with only a vague notion that it would lead to a coherent view of government's role in society. Gradually it dawned upon them that when some basic principle is suggested on which interactions between people can be based, or some basic assumption about human nature can be deduced, advice on government's role in society usually, but not always, follows.

The basic assumption about human nature in Pareto's Republic is that people ceaselessly seek out their private interest. The principle upon which they act to maximize this interest is the exchange of private property rights. So why do we need government in the Republic?

In Pareto's Republic government may need to intervene when individuals, acting on their own initiative, are unable to create systems of property rights that impartially help to resolve disputes over how resources should be used. In simple language, people may need an umpire to enforce the rules of the property rights "game" impartially because some may be tempted to play dirty and settle things by force rather than by offering money.

That umpire is called government. In practice and theory, government is that institution in society which holds a monopoly on coercive force. Since Pareto's Republic is based on property rights, the most basic function of government is to protect these rights by suppressing expressions of force by private individuals. This is the meaning of rule of law, and as we saw in the previous chapter, if the law is allowed to favour some over others, then force rather than agreement can become the determining factor in social accounting. When this happens, social accounts can fall seriously out of balance.

Even with a government ready to enforce the law of property evenly, there may be cases in which it is simply impossible to assign property. How do you give someone the exclusive right over a school of fish that may roam the ocean in complete ignorance that they belong to a human? Then there are the great projects that benefit everyone, but for which no entrepreneur could charge. If you lit public streets with lamps, how would you charge passersby for the service? Fish cannot be assigned to an owner nor can one charge for street lighting. In such cases great projects will fail to get off the ground, and people will either overexploit an open natural resource or fight each other over it. Without property rights to act as a peaceful and productive dispute resolution mechanism, some sort of official coercion might be needed to put a cap on the disagreements that arise. Submitting to government is unpleasant, but allowing private individuals to resolve their differences by force can produce a state of anarchy.

Here, then, is a possible justification for government in Pareto's Republic: to resolve disputes where property rights cannot be established and exchanged in a private market. This chapter explains that in fact this is the only justification for government. This may sound narrow and blinkered. What about help for the poor, public health care, or education for those who cannot afford it? To answer this challenge we must broaden our understanding of what property is. We will see that there are two instances in which private disputes over resources cannot be resolved peacefully between individuals. This is the case when resources belong to a common property pool such as an ocean fishery. In such cases, it is impossible to control the overexploitation of the resource by peaceful agreements between individuals. We will also see that individuals may fail to band together in great projects, known as public goods, that benefit all because it is impossible to stop some from shirking their responsibility to contribute to the project and thus "poach" on the investment others may make.

We will reach two conclusions. First, care for the poor and many other forms of government intervention we consider to be worthy on their own merits may be justified on the grounds that property rights have failed. Government may step in to produce levels of public service that simulate a Pareto-efficient outcome. Second, we will see that government should never try to hold on to any of its functions for too long. Progress in technology makes it possible in ways never before imagined to establish new private property rights. When such an advance occurs, government should abandon its stewardship of the resource in question.

The two reasons property rights fail

As previously mentioned, there are two circumstances in which property rights fail. One circumstance is the existence of a very strange sort of resource known as a "public good." (This is not to be confused with *the* public good.) A second circumstance is called "the tragedy of the commons." These two exceptions to property rights, and only these two, can undermine the peaceful, Pareto-efficient resolution of disputes. Understanding how these two circumstances challenge property rights and devising countermeasures that bring us back to Pareto efficiency was largely the work of three thinkers. In a four-page essay from 1954, Nobel Prize winning economist Paul Samuelson came up with a mathematical formula that could precisely answer how much of a public good government should provide to attain Pareto efficiency. This precision was at that time quite new in the social sciences. All previous attempts by intellectuals to define government's role dealt with generalities and left the decisions about the amount to spend to the discretion of the party or of enlightened leaders.

What distinguished Samuelson's formula from earlier thinking was not the brilliance of the analysis, but a practical proposition on how to put his idea into practice. Nicholas Kaldor and John Hicks discovered a principle showing how to convert the Samuelson formula into a workable plan consistent with Pareto optimality. Samuelson's formula needed conversion because as we shall see, on its own, it had the potential to be a tool for oppression. At around the same time as Samuelson was coming up with his formula, Garret Hardin was raising the alarm over something he called the tragedy of the commons. Hardin's essay of the same name signaled the dangers of not establishing private property rights over natural resources and became one of the most quoted academic articles of the 20th century.

Unfortunately, as in so many cases of intellectual genius, someone had already come up with Hardin's idea. That someone was H. Scott Gordon. Here is not the place to dwell on this controversy, but rather to understand how the insights of Samuelson, and Gordon and Hardin, led to the first scientific justification for the government's quest to create a Pareto-efficient society, and how in so doing, this quest also showed how to draw a precise line dividing private initiative from legitimate government coercion.

Public goods

I INDICATED AT the start of this chapter that government should intervene in the name of Pareto efficiency where the forum for agreement over property rights breaks down. This breakdown is evident in the case of so-called public goods. Economists define a public good as one that you and I must consume together in a non-rivalrous manner, and from whose consumption neither of us may be excluded. In economic jargon, public goods are non-rivalrous and non-excludable. As with many economic definitions meant for the specialist, to make sense, this one calls for a few examples.

We take night life in the streets for granted, but until the 19th century, dark was a time to slam the dead bolts shut and cower in bed. The *Gentleman's Magazine,* a publication popular in the 1700s for its eclectic mix of current events, science, and poetry, summarized the general feeling with the statement, "dark was the night, it was that hour, when terror reigns in fullest power. When, as the learned of old have said, the yawning grave gives up her dead." This was a slight exaggeration perhaps, but one that conveyed the fear of crime that rose as the sun fell. With the discovery of how to turn coal into a combustible gas in the early 1800s, illuminating streets became feasible, yet the promise this offered of banishing fear from the streets at night remained elusive. Companies supplied gas to factories and private properties that could be metered, but gas lamps were largely absent from city streets. With the exception of burglars, most people would have benefited from lighting and would have been willing to pay something for the service. Private firms did not provide lighting to public areas because they had no way to collect money from the person walking through a public street at three o'clock in the morning. This was a shame because street lighting had a remarkable quality. What any one person consumed did not detract from another's consumption. Once a system of street lights was built, one person or a thousand people could enjoy it without any change in one person's consumption. Street lighting offered society a service that all could consume without rivalry or argument. Private goods, in contrast, are rivalrous. What I consume of them reduces what you may consume. A sandwich is rivalrous because every bite I take means a bite less for you. No such conflict arises with street lighting.

Another example of a public good is the legal "infrastructure" that secures property rights. By definition, secure property rights can have only one protector. A property rights regime that guarantees Pareto-efficient peace cannot be "consumed locally," that is, different laws cannot apply to different individuals concerning the same property. If there were to be a different law for each person, then local property rights would be just a fancy term for the arbitrary use of force to settle disputes over resources. For a property rights regime to work efficiently, it must work "globally," that is, be applied equally to all. This idea of global application is the cornerstone of the rule of law. The property rights regime that emerges from the rule of law spreads its benefits indivisibly on all.

Living in a society that has secure property rights is like walking along a well-lit street at night. The glow is not diminished by the presence of an extra walker.

Prisoner's dilemma

THAT A GOOD is consumed without rivalry, as is the case with street lighting, is not a sufficient reason for government to intervene in its production or distribution. People who watch a movie in the theatre do so jointly, each without detracting from the consumption of another (unless excessively high headwear is involved). There seems to be no problem with having the private sector provide this service. Street lighting, on the other hand, is a candidate for government attention because, for technological reasons, or because of constitutional guarantees of privacy, it is not possible to track people in the streets and send them a bill for their presence there at night.

When people are not obliged to pay directly for a service or good, a "free-rider" mentality may develop and the funds needed to maintain the service may dry up, much to the detriment of all, including those who free rode. The free-rider mentality develops because of a phenomenon known as the prisoner's dilemma. The origins of the term are not important. What the dilemma describes are situations in which people who follow their personal interests end up producing collective calamities that serve no one. If street lighting depended on voluntary contributions then the individual following his or her best interest would reason as follows. If I free-ride on the funding of others, I will enjoy the street lighting but will not have paid for it. Conversely, if I believe no one else will contribute to the fund, there is also no point in me spending my money. So no matter what the strategy of other "players" in this game, my best strategy is not to contribute and hope that if the project gets built, I will get a free ride. This type of thinking cascades until the burden on remaining individuals willing to give charitably may be such that the street lighting project founders. The irony here is that everyone is worse off in this case than if they could have found some means of all binding themselves to giving to the fund.

Public goods are sometimes in short supply due to free riders, but there are exceptions. If a sufficient number of people are united in a charitable enterprise, they will not reason as free riders and will voluntarily band together to get the big jobs done. Voluntary donations of money and effort by members of every social standing built the gothic cathedral of Chartres. In his book *Civilization*, Kenneth Clarke describes how both high-born ladies and charwomen carried stones on their backs for miles to be set before master craftsmen working on what was then and remains a miracle of architecture. The tradition of charity among all economic classes in the West continues to this day and constitutes an important part of modern economies.

Yet despite the powerful expressions of charity in today's society, the very size of that society gives rise to the threat that free riding will be a problem that may stop the really big jobs from getting done. As mentioned recently, the foundering of collective effort due to free riding is one variant of what game theorists call the prisoner's dilemma. The dilemma exists when an individual does not have either law or custom to help him or her bond with others in mutually beneficial agreements. In the absence of such bonds, the logic of personal greed leads to a collective breakdown which leaves everyone worse off than if they had cooperated. Government can prevent this breakdown by forcing us to pay the taxes needed to get the public goods projects built.

The idea that government has the power to coerce us sounds sinister, but in the case of public goods, everyone agrees to be coerced so that they can escape the prisoner's dilemma and enjoy the fruits of collective action. A folk tale in economics illustrates the point. Cruising down China's Yangtze River in the 1920s, a Western woman observed a barge being towed by men struggling on the embankment under the ministrations of a whip-yielding headman. "I thought you had done away with slavery," the tourist commented to her guide, to which he responded, "Madam, they are not slaves, but rather the employers of the whip master." To ensure that all pulled their weight, the men hired a supervisor to goad them into putting equal effort into pulling their jointly owned barge up the river. What we must not forget in telling this story is that the men towing the barge had a variety of whip masters to choose from. For governments to provide public goods without abusing their coercive powers, public choice of government is also needed, as will be illustrated with greater precision in this and following chapters.

Samuelson's rule

IF WE CAN overcome the prisoner's dilemma, we must then ask how much of a public good to provide. In the case of private goods, this is not a question we need to ponder because the private market figures out this level according to the second welfare theorem. In the case of a non-excludable good, as public goods are, private property rights are not feasible, so neither is a market in which individuals reveal their preferences and costs of production and reach deals that no one else can beat—the very essence of Pareto-efficiency. In the case of public goods, government needs some idea of preferences and costs. But public goods are also non-rivalrous, and this adds an additional layer of difficulty in figuring out the efficient level of public good. Paul Samuelson solved the puzzle of reaching this Pareto-efficient level in his famous four-page missive, *The Pure Theory of Public Expenditure*. He applied the logic of market equilibrium for rivalrous private goods, to non-rivalrous goods, and discovered that it was grossly Pareto-inefficient. He then borrowed from the Hicks-Kaldor compensation principle to reassure us that his rule had the potential to be Pareto-efficient. This may all seem like a debate about how many angels can fit on the head of a pin, but as we will see, this was the debate that helped unite the science of economics with politics, and helped to clarify what the proper limits to government action should be in Pareto's Republic.

The logic of Samuelson's rule is simple. Keep increasing the level of a public good as long as the sum of what people are willing to pay exceeds the cost of providing that increase. To see this, consider a public singer visiting a village of ten residents where everyone listens to the performance. The service is non-rivalrous because one person's enjoyment does not detract from that of any other. For this singer's service, each villager might be willing to contribute a bowl of soup, although the singer would be happy with just one. Clearly, some level of payment could be found to improve everyone's well-being, so there is room for improvement. A similar, second singer willing to accept only one bowl of soup could accompany the first, but now the villagers would only be willing to contribute half a bowl of soup each, as the novelty of performance has started to fade. This is a Pareto-improving addition, but there is still room to improve both the lot of singers and villagers. Singers should be brought in until no villager is willing to contribute more than a tenth of a bowl of soup to the last one. Bring in a further singer beyond this previous one and the sum of what people are willing to pay would fall below one bowl of soup and no Pareto-improving exchange would be possible. Once no Pareto improvements are possible, you have attained Pareto efficiency.

And that is the Samuelson rule for achieving the Pareto-efficient level of a non-rivalrous good or service in its simplest form. Just keep increasing the level while the sum that all people are willing to contribute together is still more than the cost of providing that unit. Stop increasing the non-rivalrous good or service at the point where joint willingness to pay is equal to the extra cost of provision.

I say that is the rule in its simplest form because a wrinkle seems to arise when villagers differ in their willingness to pay but are all forced to contribute the same amount of soup. With varying degrees of willingness to pay, Samuelson's rule could easily violate Pareto efficiency. If you followed Samuelson's rule, you could run into a situation where one villager was willing to pay half a bowl of soup less than the admission price and another was willing to pay a full bowl of soup more. In this case, the rule would say keep increasing the number of singers because the sum of extra willingness to pay exceeds the extra cost by a half, even though one villager would clearly suffer, and by his or her suffering, strip Samuelson's rule of its Pareto efficiency. The way to turn this seeming violation of Pareto efficiency into a win-win situation is to have the more enthusiastic villager compensate the less enthusiastic villager for his loss. He can still perform this compensation and come out ahead because his gain from the increase is bigger than the other villager's loss.

All that matters for Samuelson's rule to work is that some change to the supply of a public good be such that the sum of what some people are willing to pay above their tax price for the increase exceeds what some other people would have to be compensated because their tax "price" is superior to what they are willing to pay. Basically, if some benefit greatly, the windfall can be spread to others. The possibility of compensating losers is known as the Hicks-Kaldor compensation principle and this is what allows Samuelson's rule to lead us towards the Pareto-efficient provision of a non-rivalrous good or service.

Compensation is also at the heart of Pareto efficiency in private markets for rivalrous goods and services. In that case, the search for Pareto efficiency can be left to individuals because rivalrous goods are privately consumed. Each individual can seek out others who can compensate him or her with a cash payment in exchange for the good and need not take into account the use of this good on others, because rivalrous goods do not directly affect anyone else's well-being in the way that non-rivalrous goods do. The good passes from hand to hand until it finds the person willing to offer the greatest compensation for its use. No such individual process is possible for non-rivalrous, non-excludable goods, but the hope among economists is that Hicks-Kaldor compensation could be the practical way of making Samuelson's rule work in the real world. All it would take is information on what people are willing to pay.

The informational challenge to Samuelson's rule

PRIVATE MARKETS EXPOSE what people are willing to pay, and what producers can charge if pushed to the wall by competition from rivals. Government does not have access to such an information revelation mechanism, as Hayek pointed out, because it cannot exploit the increasing returns to the private search for information open solely to the individual and revealed only in a competitive market situation. Put more plainly, you have to basically be in the situation to understand what the value of a reallocation of resources is.

No power, however august or highly placed can out-think the man or woman on the street buying purse straps or remaindered books because *experience is knowledge*. Imagine a spy-satellite filming two men talking. What are they saying? Did they pass between them a book or a cheque? More importantly, what do both feel is the value of continuing their meetings and exchanges? This is true in the case of rivalrous goods and services, which we examined at length in the previous chapter, and it is also cripplingly true in the case of non-rivalrous goods and services. Yet whereas government could help a society attain Pareto efficiency in the case of rivalrous resources by creating and protecting private property rights, it has no such a possibility when it comes to non-rivalrous goods which happen also to be non-excludable.

Non-excludable, non-rivalrous resources are called public goods and cannot be supplied by the private market due to the free-rider problem even though there is a need for them. It seems we are stuck with the need for government to provide these goods, and even though we know the correct formula, courtesy of Paul Samuelson, we are missing one very important piece of information: willingness to pay. In the market for private, rivalrous goods, this information comes out through the competitive process. In the case of a public good there is no competitive process because due to the lack of excludability there is no market; consequently, there is no readily available measure of willingness to pay, which means that government faces a major problem in implementing the Hicks-Kaldor compensation criterion, the basis for the practical Pareto-efficient implementation of the Samuelson rule.

Knowing what your customers are willing to pay is an ongoing challenge to private entrepreneurs. Those that get the calculation right thrive. Those that miscalculate disappear from the market. Economist Armen Alchian suggested that trial and error by entrepreneurs is part of an evolutionary process that leads private markets to Pareto efficiency in a sort of contest to determine who is fittest to survive. Entrepreneurial ventures in private markets are dying and being born all the time. Their stories provide surviving entrepreneurs with constantly updated lessons on the needs of the market. It is this process that helps push society to Pareto efficiency. No such stories are available for public goods because there are no markets, only the stories professors of economics tell. Is there no solution to this problem?

The problem with implementing the public goods rule is that government has trouble determining what people want the way a market does in order to divine how much they wish to pay. Government must learn about the needs of people through elections, or in the case of an autocratic regime, through the murmuring of courtiers and the din of rioting in the streets. Even elections can be an unreliable guide to public good demand because of the separation of the act of voting from the obligation to pay for what one is getting. Government agents might ask people directly, but the response might not be well thought-out because nothing is directly at stake for the person. The answer could be exaggerated if the person thinks others will pay most of the tax, or understated if the person thinks a disproportionate amount of the tax will fall on him or her. There is no getting around this challenge. Governments cannot gather information continually as do markets because governments are big. They change seldom by comparison with firms. So gathering accurate information is a problem.

Economists and political scientists agonized for decades over the question of how government might get to know what people were willing to pay for public goods. Looking directly at private markets to see how much people were willing to pay for certain goods was not much help because private markets failed to produce or price public goods such as street lighting, national security, a legal system, and disease control. The data were simply not there.

Some hope for pricing public goods came from the work of economist Sherwin Rosen. In the 1970s, Rosen invented "hedonic analysis," which, under very strict theoretical conditions, could take something like the price of a house, and unravel it to show how street lighting, parks, and other public amenities contributed to its value. By isolating how much of the benefit of a public good seeps into housing value, hedonic analysis could indirectly measure the value of public goods. Yet the method was also plagued by lack of relevant data on housing characteristics and some very strict theoretical conditions were needed to make it a practical tool. It was a hot topic in economics in the 1970s but seems to not have had much impact on the science of pricing government services, perhaps because of all the "ifs" involved. Later in the 1970s, Swiss researchers, most notably Bruno Frey and Werner Pommerehne, thought they had come upon a solution to the problem of pricing public goods. They argued that one could draw inferences about willingness to pay in the political market in the same way as one could from the private market. Look at what voters are willing to pay in taxes for different levels of public goods, they said. If you find similar communities but with different tax levels and different levels of public goods consumption, you might be able to build some notion of the relation between what people were willing to pay in taxes for a given level consumed.

It was a business of connecting the dots. The first dot was the community with low taxes and low public goods. The second dot was the community with slightly higher taxes and more public goods. By connecting the dots you could establish how much people were willing to pay for a certain level of public good. Once you had this information on willingness to pay, you could compare it to the costs of providing the public good, and keep providing that good as long as the costs were less than the willingness to pay. Here, then, seemed to be a heuristic, or rule-of-thumb for supplying the Pareto-optimal level of a public good.

The statistical picture these researchers painted was clouded by the possibility that the link between the level of public goods supplied and what people were paying was only a surface impression of linkage and not a causal relation. Perhaps people paid more for higher levels of public goods because some unaccounted force, such as a rise in wealth, had given communities the ability to ask for more. There are statistical techniques for filtering out or "controlling" for the effect of a third factor interfering with causal interpretations, but these techniques rely for their effectiveness on assumptions that are so tenuous that they can be thought of as exercises in divination. Yet the more fundamental objection to this approach was the simplest. How do you know that the governments in the other communities got the calculation right? If they did not provide the correct level of public goods for a given tax price, you were basing your government decisions upon the mistaken premises of other governments.

The first Queen Elizabeth said, "I have no desire to make windows into men's souls." Yet what else can economists do but peep into souls in order to prescribe optimal levels of public goods? Or so it seemed until, gradually, researchers began to understand the link between Samuelson's formula and the work of Duncan Black that has since come to be called the "median voter theorem."

The median voter model in relation to Samuelson

ONE WAY OUT of the problem of using community level data, or hedonic analysis, to divine demand for public goods was to build a model that could predict who decides policies in a democracy. The most popular model so far has been that of the median voter, which Duncan Black produced in a 1948 article entitled, *On the Rationale of Group Decision-making*. Black's model marks the start of the modern mathematical era of the study of government and excellent reading on this can be found in *The Encyclopedia of Public Choice*. Black's work also formed a bridge between elections and questions of the Pareto-efficient supply of public goods, and for this reason it should be considered the foundational research piece that united politics and economics under the banner of Pareto-efficient thinking.

Black's theory says that if the debate over public goods is simple enough to be put on a left-to-right scale, such as would be the case with military, or health expenditures, and if a few other highly technical assumptions about people's preferences hold, then the level of public good a government provides will be that which is preferred by the median voter. No one has ever met this voter, but in theory, he or she sits in the middle of the desired level of public good of all other voters, which means that slightly fewer than fifty percent want more than the median voter, and slight fewer than fifty percent want less. The median voter decides elections.

A politician may propose a level of a public good which is greater than what three-quarters of voters want. A rival could win the election by proposing a level which is greater than what only two-thirds of voters want. He would win because his position is closer to what most people want than is the position of the first candidate. Both candidates know this game and gravitate to the position of the voter who sits in the middle of the crowd. If for each person willing to pay a certain amount less than the median voter there is another person willing to pay the same amount more, then the distribution of preferences around the median is said to be symmetric. With symmetric distributions, the median also turns out to be the average. To see this, consider three people. The first is willing to pay $1 for the public good, the next willing to pay $2, and the third willing to pay $3. The average of these three amounts is $2, which is precisely the median voter's willingness to pay.

This long chain of reasoning leads to a profound insight. If you multiply the tax price for the public good which results from the median voter's preferences by the number of people, you get the sum of the tax dollars people are willing to pay for the public good at the level actually supplied. Provided the tax price per unit of public good reflects the cost of producing an additional unit, then the election results in a government that follows Samuelson's rule. Put more simply, if the median voter represents the average voter, then you get public goods geared toward the average person. By a mathematical quirk, that average can also coincide with Samuelson's rule for the optimal provision of a public good.

Finding that the median voter's preferences can lead to the Pareto-efficient amount of public good being produced seems to do away with government's need to worry about calculating the voter's demand for public goods. All that is needed to produce the right amount of public good is taxation and a competitive election, just as competition and property rights were the only ingredients needed for markets to produce the Pareto-efficient level of private goods. Never before had intellectuals forged such a sharp argument for justifying government intervention as they had with Samuelson's rule grafted to Black's median voter theorem.

Despite the elegance of Samuelson and Black's analysis, we should not allow ourselves to apply their insights without also understanding the limitations of these insights. The Samuelson rule only applies to public goods, that is, projects that have the potential to serve all people in a non-rivalrous manner. These are the types of government intervention that unite people by working in the interests of all. Samuelson's rule does not apply to the selfish redistribution of income such as might happen when a cynical interest group gets a law passed that protects it from competition and allows it to raise prices at the expense of consumers. Nor does it preserve any link with the median voter theorem when property rights are not protected by law. In a democracy that has no property protection, voting can become the means by which some groups rob the resources of other groups through taxation and redistribution. This is the exact opposite of the peace of Pareto. For us to have faith that Samuelson's rule can work through the medium of the median voter theorem, some economic prerequisites to democracy need to be present. We shall see what these are two chapters from now, but you may not be surprised to know that the most important prerequisite is the protection of property rights.

The tragedy of the commons

PUBLIC GOODS LEAD to too little private initiative to produce them because their non-excludable character means that people can free ride on the service provided. With too many free riders and too few paying customers, such a service would fail. There is an opposite problem. Sometimes people provide not too little, but too much effort. In the case of public goods, people free ride, or under-participate in providing the good because they benefit without paying the costs. In the opposite problem, people provide too much effort because they benefit from their effort without taking into account the cost this imposes on others. This is the diametrically opposite, but logically close relative of public goods, and it is called the problem of the common property resource.

Sometimes property is impossible to assign and the consequences of that may be the devastation of some natural resource. As H. Scott Gordon writes, "Significantly, land tenure is found to be 'common' only in those cases where the hunting resource is migratory over such large areas that it cannot be regarded as husbandable by the society" (page 134). In 19th century America, close to a hundred million buffalo roamed the Plains. Much of the Plains was unclaimed, and even the parts that were claimed could not contain the buffalo. Property rights were impossible to assign. Railroads reached the plains in the 1870s and brought with them hunters who would kill as many buffalo as possible and ship their hides back east by rail, and farmers who used the new invention of barbed wire to block the buffalo from their lands. By 1876, the buffalo were nearly extinct. The loss of nearly a hundred million buffalo in a few years was clearly not to the advantage of hunters. Rather than slaughtering hundreds of head a day, the hunter might have preferred to keep the buffalo in captivity where he could exploit them at his or her leisure, not just the skin, but also the meat and bones and the potential to generate offspring. This is the strategy of cultivation that modern farmers seeking to revive the buffalo have adopted, and in so doing they have multiplied the buffalo to levels unimagined by Theodore Roosevelt, the first American president to take nature conservation seriously. Yet without the property rights that would allow them to take a long-term view of the buffalo, hunters had no choice but to slaughter the entire herd.

The buffalo were victims of the pernicious logic of the prisoner's dilemma, which, as we have seen, allows collective insanity to percolate out of the rational behaviour of individuals. Any show of restraint by one hunter might not have been matched by other hunters. Hunters who might have cared about the future of the buffalo were pushed to behave like out-of-control predators for fear that others might profit from their restraint. All hunters might have wanted to preserve the herd, but none could afford to act in a way that would do so. As H. Scott Gordon wrote

> The blade of grass that the manorial cowherd leaves behind is valueless to him, for tomorrow it may be eaten by another's animal; the oil left under the earth is valueless to the driller, for another may legally take it; the fish in the sea are valueless to the fisherman, because there is no assurance that they will be there for him tomorrow if they are left behind today" (page 135).

Without some mechanism to bind the separate strands of their interests into a common strategy, the unregulated pursuit of individual self-interest leads to a devastation of the common property resource that no one would have wished for. Such is the essence of the prisoner's dilemma.

Garret Hardin called this senseless squandering of resources that arises from the prisoner's dilemma "the tragedy of the commons" and laid down a challenge to researchers: figure out a practical means by which to avert this tragedy. A group of thinkers mixing mathematics, economics, sociology, and jurisprudence took up the challenge. They included political scientist Elinor Ostrom, who won a Nobel Prize in economics for her efforts. Inspired by Gordon and Hardin, they compiled a large number of case studies showing how small groups of people learned to cooperate to avoid the tragedy of the commons. They discovered that in small groups, community censure, local mores, intermarriage, clan loyalty, and friendship are all reasonably successful attempts to conquer the prisoner's dilemma and its manifestation in the despoliation of nature. The trick in all these cases is to devise some means by which people can take into account the long-term consequences of their actions on others—and vice versa.

Despite their initial enthusiasm, the researchers found that these informal solutions quickly break down as the size of the group increases and people lose touch with each other. In small groups your peers hold you to account. In large groups there are few peers. In large societies laws governing the protection and exchange of property are what hold people to account. Private property eliminates the tragedy of the commons by its permanence, the very thing that was lacking in relations between hunters of the buffalo. Property rights carry with them a guarantee that the terms of some agreement, such as a lease, will not change even if the identity of the lessor or lessee changes. Nor will the terms change if the lessor decides to threaten the lessee. Contracts and the impartial protection of the law give stability to relations between people moderated by property. Such stability was absent from relations between buffalo hunters because of the transient and lawless nature of their venture.

Taming the tragedy of the commons was the first great challenge governments faced on the road to modernity. The commons in question were to some extent forests and lakes, but far more importantly, the land that peasants tilled, and the income that city dwellers earned. In his fascinating book, *Violence in Early Modern Europe 1500-1800*, Julius Ruff describes how brigands and soldiers preyed on these riches almost without restraint, as would hunters exploiting a common property resource. Much of the devastation of property was due not to foreign invaders, but to one's own military. Until the late 17th century, governments had difficulty feeding and housing their armies. A military campaign did most of its damage off the battlefield by the disorganized and destructive manner in which soldiers foraged for their food, either in foreign lands or while tearing out a vegetable garden while billeted in a private home.

A Dutch painting from this period entitled *Peasant Sorrow* by David Vinckboons shows soldiers glutting themselves at the expense of peasants looking on in shock. A second painting entitled *Peasant Joy* shows these same villagers armed with axes and bug-eyed with rage driving the military moochers from their homes. When predation by armies intensified, peasants became disheartened with tending fields that had essentially become common property. The logic of the prisoner's dilemma drove entire communities to join bands of brigands, which in turn compounded the common property problem. During the Thirty Years' War, large parts of Germany and central Europe became, in essence, a vast common property resource in which everything was for everyone's taking. Tales from these times speak of famine and plagues that spread amongst populations debilitated by starvation.

Historian William McNeill suggested in his book *Plagues and Peoples,* and its sequel, *The Pursuit of Power,* that through most of history, armies resembled an endemic disease, perpetually weakening and slowing the progress of their own societies. Governments began to control this disease by diverting the predatory tendencies of their armies away from their own people. Durable foods that could be carried on the march, such as smoked meats and compact high-calorie meals, kept the military "disease-parasite" from feeding on local populations. So did the military invention of canned food. Financial innovations allowed government to contract with private suppliers who could meet an army at regular points on its route. Administrative advances allowed quartermasters to organize long baggage trains that carried tents and fuel so that armies could maintain their soldiers in the field rather than billeting them in private houses. Between wars, governments learned that housing soldiers in barracks was less expensive in the long run than the destruction and ill will wrought by traditional systems of billeting.

By being open to advances in learning that allowed them literally to remove their armies from the fields, governments of the 18th century created vast zones of stable private property for perhaps the first time since the Roman Empire. The enhanced protection of property allowed entrepreneurs to exploit advances in both production and agricultural technology and eventually helped the industrial revolution.

The benefits of inefficient government

IN ALMOST EVERY instance where government stepped in to avert the tragedy of the commons, it did so because of technological advances in administration and measurement. Any government that was acting coherently and was not itself in the grips of the prisoner's dilemma sought to tame whatever tragedy of the commons it could whenever the means arose, simply because of the money amounts involved.

Initially governments tried to become proprietors, making forests and some cities royal preserves, but as techniques of taxation evolved it made more sense to leave newly defined and protected properties in the hands of private individuals. The private sector specialized in developing the former common property whilst government specialized in its coercive function of collecting taxes. Direct money profits, rather than the diffuse and hard-to-measure benefits of public goods drove governments to tame the commons.

The search for enhanced tax revenues, which led to the closing of the commons, meshed the interests of despotic governments quite nicely with the interests of citizens. This confluence of interests revealed why it makes sense for governments to divest themselves of the management and financing of resources whenever possible.

The reason for wishing government to convert the commons to private property, when technology allows, rests on the principle of the division of labour. The division of labour is an insight often attributed to Adam Smith, but is of much older intellectual lineage. It states that identical workers in some cooperative venture can increase their efficiency in ways mutually profitable to both if they are allowed to specialize in circumscribed tasks.

Smith gave the example of pin makers, some of whom focused on making the head of the pin while others focused on the body. By limiting themselves to narrow tasks and becoming good at them, a cooperative of workers could produce far more than if each worker had to produce the entire pin by himself. The gains in efficiency from dividing labour would be even greater if each worker was born with some innate, focused ability which exceeded that of others.

Smith's insights are general enough for our purposes to be applied beyond the factory floor. The most obvious implication is that there are gains to society from allowing government and the private sector to specialize in different activities. What distinguishes government from the private sector is that government can dictate how people must act, whereas the people in the private sector must rely on persuasion, perhaps by means of an institution such as property. Smith would say, allow government to specialize in the manipulation of coercive power while allowing the private sector to specialize in persuasion.

A government whose objective was Pareto efficiency would specialize in finding coercive methods that best allow people to pursue their own interests while not harming others. The private sector could then specialize in the search for innovative ways to use property. While Smith spoke of efficiency, his idea implies that everyone must also be relatively inefficient at tasks for which they are neither suited nor specialized. We want government to be inefficient at some things so that it will be more efficient at others. This is how society exploits the division of labour between government and the private sector.

There are, of course, some commons that cannot be converted to private property. As yet we have no way of determining whom the air belongs to, or who can claim fish in the ocean, except in the crudest of senses. These types of common property can be protected by government limits on pollution and quotas on fishing. Here the question of what level of quota to set might be inferred from market data on how much people are willing to pay for the resource in question.

Remember that Pareto efficiency relies on exploiting resources in such a way that their cost does not exceed how much people are willing to pay for them. If costs go beyond benefit, there is no "surplus" to be divided in a Pareto-improving way in society. In principle, government could decide the level of the quota by studying the demand for the fish in question and learning about the costs of harvesting the fish. Demand and cost are the raw data a market uses to generate a Pareto-efficient level of output, so it is conceivable that government could simulate Pareto efficiency with the help of these data, but that is not a task for which it is suited. Government in this case should think of itself as a steward waiting impatiently for its ward to grow up. While the natural commons are an important and ongoing challenge to developing countries, in developed countries, with the prominent exceptions of fisheries and air pollution, the challenge is self-imposed. It lies in protecting the "fiscal commons."

The fiscal commons

IN DEVELOPED COUNTRIES, the public has shown an aversion to direct fees for chargeable services in education, health, and the use of highways. Without fees, governments must find some way of limiting access to public services because free access always produces excess demand. Excess in the sense that people are incited to consume the service to a level where what they are willing to pay for it is far less than the cost of providing it. This sort of excess puts society's social accounts into the red, which is not a prescription for sustained prosperity or stability. The alternative to charging for a publicly provided good has generally been to impose a quota on consumption. Politicians interested in keeping their jobs deny that they impose quotas on these services. It is unwise to arouse the public's

annoyance by upsetting its belief in open and boundless access, but the unpleasant logic of common property forces governments to "shape" demand by limiting access. The resulting congestion and long waiting lines for publicly provided
services follow from government's attempts to protect the fiscal commons by
imposing quotas. The fiscal commons is a challenge to Pareto efficiency because
consumption quotas prevent people from realizing their potential in three ways.

The first inefficiency of consumption quotas arises if we do not allow them to
be traded. A patient with a torn knee ligament who must wait nine months for
knee surgery may lose his or her job. A retired patient with the same injury at
the front of the queue might be able to wait nine months without much bother.
Both could gain if the employed patient paid the retired patient to change places
in the queue. Tradable "queue" quotas would be a remedy for the arbitrary way
in which waiting lists order their subjects. Tradable quotas already exist for some
fisheries, and even for pollution. In the case of fisheries, inefficient ships that
damage too much of their catch cannot make much profitable use of the quota,
so they sell it to the efficient ships that cause less wastage.

In the case of pollution, government issues permissible emission levels to
firms, which they can then trade. An inefficient firm is one that pollutes heavily
for each unit of output it produces. It would rapidly use up its quota and produce only a small amount. Instead of going this route, it would prefer to sell the
quota to firms that produce less pollution per unit produced. In this way, tradable
emissions quotas allow an industry to produce the greatest amount of product
for the fixed level of pollution that government has deemed acceptable. So far,
governments have been too timid or unimaginative to apply their experience of
issuing tradable pollution and fishing quotas to other areas, such as health care
queues or other services.

The second problem with consumption quotas for freely provided goods is
that of insufficient information about what people are willing to pay. By not testing the market with different levels of fees, government deprives itself of information about what different individuals are willing to pay for a variety of services.

Socialist economist Oscar Lange argued that a centrally planned economy
could get all the information it needed about satisfying demand by looking at
how inventories were behaving. If inventories for clothes were falling, then it was
time to make more clothes. At a very crude level, this is true, if we are talking
perhaps about grey Mao Zedong uniforms once worn by millions of Chinese.
But what about the clothes that have not yet been designed and that exist only
in the imaginations of their potential creators? Without a market to test a wide

variety of designs and to determine by survival of the fittest which design is to be produced by whom, those who live under consumption quotas are deprived of goods and services customized to their tastes and needs.

As in the case of public goods, it is not sufficient simply to ask people how much they are willing to pay and what kinds of services they want. In opinion surveys, talk is cheap. The best evidence for what people will pay arises when money actually changes hands. Without such credible market feedback on consumer preferences, government has little choice but to provide a standardized service. The shortage of information may be as acute for those services that are freely provided as it is for public goods where we saw there were no private market examples to go by.

Freely provided services, such as health care in mildly socialist countries such as Canada and the Czech Republic, can be complex. It does not help the government to look at how the private sector in other countries is balancing needs against means, simply because such information cannot be culled at long distances. The lack of information about customer needs is why when one enters a public hospital or school, one is struck by the uniformity and blandness of the settings as well as by the almost complete lack of a consumer service ethic. People who work in these institutions are not incompetent, nor indifferent. They simply have few signals that reliably indicate how the needs of their clients vary.

The third problem with divisible, publicly-provided rivalrous goods such as health care is likely the most vexing. Unlike true public goods, which are non-rivalrous, by their very nature public health care, public pensions, and similar products generate conflict in society. Think of what the words mean. Can publicly-provided rivalrous goods be anything but a source of rivalry? These are resources up for grabs, idling in a government preserve like antelope grazing before the excited gaze of predators. Government by definition is an organization that holds a monopoly on coercion. Whatever stands in its pasture becomes the prize gained in the struggle for control of government. Governments that socialize private, rivalrous goods find themselves in a vortex of social antagonisms.

By socializing decisions about private property, these governments drag us into the arena of conflict that was so well trodden in East Bloc countries. Socialism is by definition lawless because it puts all decisions about private property in public hands. In public hands, the sole and final arbiter is the strength of the ruling interest group. Socialization of divisible, rivalrous property rights is a problem that governments bring upon themselves needlessly. By diverting people from seeking cooperative solutions to society's collective problems, the socialization of private property makes each of us an enemy to the rest of us.

The lowered tone of "political discourse" that scholars have identified in recent decades may result from the socialization of private property. Problems of social conflict are attenuated when government concerns itself strictly with providing public, non-rivalrous goods and protecting the natural commons, because these issues deal with questions of collective well-being. Publicly provided rivalrous goods pit each man and woman against the other. No wonder political change has become nearly impossible in most developed countries. Too much of what could be peacefully resolved by individuals trading private property under the rule of law has been moved into the combat zone of public ownership.

So what about fairness?

I HAVE NOT mentioned fairness so far in this chapter, which may seem a major omission as most people believe that government should have some role in determining a fair division of resources. Instead, I have argued that government's only role in society is to plug gaps left when private property rights malfunction, and that even then, government should divest itself of managing these resources once privatization becomes feasible. To understand the role of fairness in Pareto's Republic, we need to distinguish between the concept's two variants.

The first variant is distributional fairness. It is a criterion for dividing society's resources separately from any decisions individuals might make. As explained in the previous chapter, distributional fairness was the major preoccupation of former East Bloc countries when they made the transition from socialism to the free market. To make the transition, governments had to transfer the bulk of their holdings into private hands. Pareto efficiency was useless as a guide because there were too many Pareto-efficient initial distributions to choose from. Countries in transition had to rely on societal notions of fairness in the transfer and they had to make sure that no individual could influence his or her own particular slice of the pie, a condition that was honoured more in the breach than in the observance.

Once they had transferred resources into private hands, these countries had to implement the second form of fairness, procedural fairness. This is a criterion for managing resources once the initial distribution is done and it can depend heavily on individual choice. The two main forms of procedural fairness available in large societies are management of resources by government officials and management by people holding private property. Having emerged from state management, transition economies naturally strove to create economies based on private property, trusting in the second theorem of welfare economics which holds that the "lump-sum" transfers they made to their people would lead to one specific Pareto-efficient outcome for society. This is an arid but correct way of saying that once you put private property into people's hands and allow them to trade freely in a market, these people will seek out and find how best to exchange their initial endowments in a Pareto-efficient manner.

The distinction between distributive and procedural fairness needs to be refined to account for the fact that chance frequently undoes any initial fair distribution governments make. The "slings and arrows of outrageous fortune" and the "heartaches and thousand natural shocks that flesh is heir to," as Shakespeare put it, are relentlessly challenging the accomplishments of static fairness.

A man's house may burn to the ground. A woman may win the lottery. Some are born with great intellectual gifts, or a passion for life, while others cannot chase off the black dog of depression. Private insurance can protect us from some disasters, but there is no policy than can shield us from all the bad knocks we may take through life, especially not in the presence of something called moral hazard.

There is an old joke about two farmers discussing insurance. The first one says that he has just bought fire and hail insurance. The second says, "I understand about the fire insurance, but how do you make it hail?" Insurance in this joke is a hazard to the farmer's morals because he or she may be tempted to burn the crop in order to collect on the policy. What is not funny is that when people act on moral hazard, they are violating the property rights of insurers in such a manner that can cause the market to collapse.

The presence of cheaters drives up the cost of insurance. The increased cost discourages some honest people from buying insurance. A vicious cycle may start because each honest person that is discouraged leaves behind an insurance market increasingly saturated with cheaters. Insurers must continue raising rates, which drives out more honest people, which in turn increases rates to the point where the market disappears. In some East European countries this is so grave a problem that no one will insure motor vehicles or business structures. The impossibility of creating sustainable property rights in some markets is not a blanket excuse to invite government to provide such insurance simply because there is no indication that government can do any better than the private market at identifying cheaters or eliminating moral hazard. The mammoth financial collapses that have followed government attempts to insure the real estate market suggest that government may in fact be the main instigator of moral hazard in society.

Government is on firmer ground in arguing that because we have a tendency to free ride on the charity of others, the private alms given may not suffice. Charity can be considered a public good in the sense that the money I give to the needy benefits not just the needy but also those who sympathize with them. In small, stable communities social pressures force people not to free ride on the charity of others, as any office worker well understands during collection drives by the office representative for the United Way or other such charities. In larger, more anonymous settings, social pressures do not suffice to stop some from riding off the charitable efforts of others. Such, then, is the setting in which government may take from some to give to others, an apparent violation of Pareto efficiency, if those others agree that sometimes the needy need a leg up that private charity cannot provide.

We can fold a layer of fairness into Pareto efficiency by arguing that if private markets fail to correct the most egregious outrages of chance, government may need to take something from nature's favourites and hand that something to its outcasts in the name of providing a public good. The challenge, of course, is to know just who these favourites are. Without such a guide, fairness may become a byword for theft and lead to discord in society, setting men and women against each other in a mockery of Pareto efficiency. In the case of help for the poor, as in the case of any other good or service, government must stay vigilant to the possibility of devolving charity to the private sector. That possibility arises when the private sector manages to overcome, or at least abate, the free-rider problem.

Pulling the ideas together

THIS CHAPTER'S MAIN idea can be summed up in a few sentences. We have seen that government is needed in Pareto's Republic in order to impose solutions that can resolve collective problems concerning property. Individuals in large groups cannot arrive at solutions to these problems by peaceful agreement because some will shirk their obligations and others will get their way by violence. Citizens are willing to give government a monopoly on the use of force, but only to the extent that this force is applied equally to everyone, a concept known as the rule of law. Without the rule of law, government gives itself over to arbitrariness and can become the tool of shirkers and predators in society. Under arbitrary government, property rights lose their power as a medium for resolving disputes. Those who control government and its monopoly of force can resolve disputes by the self-serving application of violence. Such governments also turn nature into a vast common property pool which the rulers can devastate with impunity.

The government that manages to impose the rule of law rather than martial law allows individuals to stop worrying about official kleptocrats and frees them to specialize and excel at producing something useful. Ultimately government should abandon providing a public good or protecting a commons when a technology comes along that allows the commons to be privatized, or a public good to be charged for on a pay-per-use basis. Governments that provide private goods reproduce the tragedy of the commons and forfeit the peaceful resolution of disputes made possible by private property rights.

All of the above analysis speaks to the benefits we get from government provision of services and goods. What about the costs? So far I have given the impression that if a bridge costs a million dollars to build, that is the cost. As the next chapter explains, the cost of government intervention goes beyond the simple bill in dollars and cents. The extra charge is called a deadweight loss. This is one of the most subtle concepts in economics and holds a special place in calculating how government should enhance Pareto efficiency.

TAXES   5

W HEN PEOPLE SAY THAT TAXES are a necessary evil, they are
speaking the language of Pareto efficiency, perhaps without
knowing they are doing so. Taxes are necessary because public
goods such as street lighting, national defense, and the legal system cannot be charged for directly due to their non-excludable character, as discussed in the last chapter. Government needs to charge for these services
indirectly by levying taxes that go into the government treasury. This tax
money can then pay for the protection of property rights and common
property resources, which, as we saw, are necessary prerequisites to obtaining Pareto efficiency.

Yet taxes can also be to some degree evil. The simple act of taxation, considered separately from the benefits of the public goods they finance, is a
direct threat to Pareto efficiency. Taxes discourage what once were Pareto-
efficient private purchases and guide people into unproductive pursuits
merely to avoid paying the levies. On the walls of some British and Canadian
houses from the 19th century you can see the outlines of what were windows.
People bricked them over to avoid the "window tax." Purely in response to
the tax, people defaced their homes and opted to lurk in domestic shadows,
in as stark a retreat from Pareto efficiency as you can find.

More commonplace effects of taxes are to discourage people from entering into exchanges that would have been mutually profitable. Taxes discourage people from buying and merchants from selling. They discourage busi-
nesspeople from investing, and workers from upgrading their skills. Taxes
do this by putting a wedge between what someone is willing to pay and the
other person is willing to accept in payment. Before the imposition of a
goods and services tax, the carpenter and I may have agreed that $20 was
an acceptable hourly wage, but after the tax is introduced, the carpenter will
have to ask me for more money. The tax has come between our mutually
acceptable arrangement and I will cut back on my use of his or her services.

The problem that governments face is that of trying to enhance Pareto efficiency by providing their citizens with public goods while at the same time keeping down the disruptions to Pareto efficiency from raising the taxes needed to buy those goods. A tale of two countries illustrates this principle.

Colbert and the rise of efficient taxation

In 1661, Louis xiv started to build the world's grandest palace near the village of Versailles from which his Bourbon clan would impose its will on Europe for three generations. In 1886, Mad King Ludwig of Bavaria began an architectural quest of equally breathless audacity. It brought him abdication and likely assassination. Ludwig drained his coffers and borrowed heavily from the state to finance a building spree that ended with an attempt to reproduce the palace of Versailles on a desolate island in the middle of a Bavarian lake. Though a strong swimmer, he was found shortly thereafter drowned in knee-deep water. France and Bavaria remain proud of these structures, even though historians tend to view both palaces as symbols of royal excess.

The economic view is not to judge these architectural tableaux by their appearance, but to consider how much disruption the financing of these palaces caused in people's lives. Louis XIV was able to finance Versailles and secure Bourbon power for a further hundred years because the French knew how to devise efficient systems of taxation that spread taxes evenly over many people and also over time, thereby lightening the load the average individual had to carry. King Ludwig, on the other hand, knew little of efficient taxation. He concentrated his energies on his pharaonic projects and on carousing with his servants, rather than listening to the counsel of his expert advisors who warned against debt and fractious debates about who should pay it. Behind his financial excesses loomed giant tax burdens that threatened economic catastrophe for Bavaria.

King Louis' minister of finance, Jean-Baptiste Colbert, considered efficient taxation as the art of "plucking the goose so as to obtain the largest amount of feathers with the least possible amount of hissing." A less elegant modern restatement is that taxes should interfere as little as possible with Pareto efficiency. As Louis demonstrated, Pareto-efficient taxation can elevate a Sun King and allow him to build outsize palaces without being deposed by his people. The ruler who ignores this principle upsets commerce and may end up floating face down in three feet of water. All of which goes to show that, not only are death and taxes inevitable, there is some indication that for dissolute royals at least, they can also go in tandem.

To pluck the goose with minimal hissing, Colbert tried not to pile too many taxes on too few people. A heavy burden on one person is far more noticeable and disruptive than a light burden spread over many. One of the chief challenges to spreading the burden evenly was that so many people evaded taxes. Colbert's efforts to force tax evaders to open their purses helped him to spread the weight of taxation evenly. This diminished the disturbances to the economy that taxation caused, and in this minimally disturbed climate, the French government was able to grow larger than that of any comparable European nation.

Colbert's insight was not unique. During the reign of King William III in the late 17th century, the British diminished the disruptiveness of their taxes by imposing excise taxes, that is, broadly based taxes collected on sales within the country. Some argue that this enabled the British to finance the armies that thwarted the French in the wars from 1688 to 1714. Three hundred years later, Nobel Prize winning economist Gary Becker and his colleague Casey Mulligan gave Colbert statistical vindication by showing that countries where taxes are spread proportionally also tend to have large governments.

Proportional spreading is what today is called a flat tax. Examples of flat taxes are unemployment insurance, contributions to public pensions, property levies, and value-added taxes. France relies on flat taxes for more than eighty percent of its revenues. The United States gets less than forty percent of its revenues from flat taxes and instead relies heavily on progressive income and corporate taxes. In France, government is large. In the US, it is small by comparison. Perhaps Americans do not like big government. Or perhaps, unlike the French, their system of taxation is not efficient enough to allow them to afford it.

Deadweight loss and efficient taxation

TODAY RESEARCHERS EXAMINING efficient taxation have clarified in modern terms what Colbert was intuitively putting into practice during the age of the Sun King. Efficient tax theory begins with the postulate that the cost to society of a tax is more than just the tax revenue that government takes in.

Pause and think about this, because it is the central idea motivating all of tax policy in pretty much every country. When government raises a million dollars in taxes, is not one million dollars the cost that people bear? The answer is no. People bear the one million dollars and then some. Economists call that "then some" the deadweight loss of the tax. To understand this we need to refine the distinction made above between the direct money cost of a tax to the person paying, and the additional sting economists call deadweight loss.

A tax has recuperable and non-recuperable components. The money government puts into its coffers is not lost. It is just a transfer from taxpayers to government that sits in some consolidated revenue fund ready to be spent on bridges or other enterprises of collective interest. This is the recuperable cost of the tax. Beyond this cost, the tax may discourage investment, consumption, work effort, and may force people to toil in the so-called underground economy, where taxes are undeclared, and government regulations on worker safety are ignored. These are all disruptions from the normal way in which economic exchanges between people would take place without taxation. The value of these lost opportunities cannot be recuperated. Economists call these deadweight costs, or more meaningfully but less commonly, excess burdens.

During the 20th century, many a fine mind in economics proposed ways in which government could devise taxes that minimize the deadweight loss to society per dollar of government revenue. This is a cryptic comment that can very easily be confused with meaning that government should minimize total deadweight losses. What is the distinction? To understand why it is that government must minimize the deadweight losses per dollar of tax revenue and not total deadweight losses, think of taxes as crops and of government as a farmer. It costs the farmer effort and material to harvest each crop. The farmer's objective is not to minimize the total cost of the harvest. He or she could do that simply by not harvesting! The objective is rather to minimize the cost for each crop brought in. In the same way, the theory of optimal taxation accepts that a government needs to raise a sum of money that can vary according to its needs: the government crop.

Taxes, no matter what their level, should minimize disruptions to Pareto efficiency for that level. In practical terms this means devising taxes that minimize the deadweight loss for each "crop" of tax revenue harvested, or more technically, to minimize the deadweight loss per unit of tax. To minimize the deadweight loss per unit of tax, government first needs to build a catalogue of these losses and get an idea of how they react to taxes, much as a farmer would need to know the costs of various fertilizers and equipment available for the planting of the crop.

Yet before we can understand the list of deadweight losses economists have compiled, we need the stark example of the effects of theft on the victim to give us a feel for deadweight loss. Theft is a very crude form of taxation, levied not by the government but by a private individual. Anyone who has had a wallet or purse stolen knows that the loss of cash is usually the smallest cause of their suffering. The real drama arises from the loss of irreplaceable pictures, *billets doux*, and from the hours spent on replacing identity documents and credit cards. These hours are lost to the individual and to society. The value of what he or she could have been doing otherwise cannot be recuperated and as such is a form of dead-weight loss. Surprisingly, the money stolen is not a deadweight loss, but rather a transfer. The dollars have not disappeared from the economy. They remain ready to pass from the thief's hands to those of unwary merchants.

Modern states emulate the thief by using force, if necessary, to relieve us of our earnings. The taxpayer considers his transfer of sums to government to be a personal loss, but as in the case of the thief, the transfer is not a loss to society because it goes into state coffers from which it may be spent. The difference between theft and taxation lies in the degree to which each generates a deadweight loss. With impersonal government taxation, one does not suffer the administrative running around and expense that accompany the pickpocket's highly personalized levy. Yet deadweight losses are not completely absent.

Taxes discourage people from entering into profitable exchanges with each other. The value of these discouraged exchanges is a deadweight loss. For instance, studies show that when government raises the income tax, some people who are not in salaried positions, such as self-employed carpenters, sign makers, and consultants, to list a few, start to work in the underground economy where they pay no tax. A deadweight loss can arise because not every consumer is willing to pay for their services without asking for a receipt for purposes of tax deduction. By limiting the pool of consumers they serve, tax evading producers cut themselves from serving potentially high-paying clients. To the carpenter this is of no concern because the evaded tax more than compensates for the extra payment he or she would receive in the legitimate market. Yet the economy is poorer because the carpenter now works for a client in the underground economy who values his or her work less than a potential client in the legitimate economy. For example, a hotel would be willing to pay the carpenter $30 an hour to improve its façade but at a fifty percent income tax the carpenter would only make $15, and so prefers to work off the books for a client willing to pay at most $20. The income tax has "re-slotted" or "displaced" people from high-yield to lower-yielding activities. The worker who evades the tax does not see things this way, because the tax has created a wedge between what the $30-an-hour employer is willing to pay and what the worker perceives to be his gain of $15 for working.

This is the manner in which taxes can blind people to the best opportunities the economy offers. Government is richer, but the economy is poorer. Even employees on a payroll may produce deadweight losses in the face of high income taxes by increasing their absenteeism. "You pretend to pay us and we pretend to work" was the slogan often used in communist countries where governments implicitly taxed their workers to excess by paying them salaries far below their productivity.

There are as many types of deadweight loss as there are taxes. The list of deadweight losses from taxation includes the lost benefits to consumers and producers from discouraged exchanges, reduced productivity due to discouraged investment in machines, the loss to society from having thousands of clever lawyers and accountants plan ways around taxes, the flow of resources away from places that produce true riches to places that produce tax rebates, and the money and effort devoted to hiding what one has from the taxperson.

No one knows for sure how many types of deadweight losses there are and spotting new problem areas is an ongoing field of research for economists. Yet what almost all known deadweight losses have in common is a property called non-linearity, and it is this property that gives rise to the theory of efficient taxation. I say "almost" because there is a curious creature economists call a lumpsum tax, more popularly known as a head-tax or poll-tax that in principle should have no deadweight loss. A lump-sum tax is one you have to pay no matter what you choose to consume, or whether you work or not. As such, it does not influence a person's calculations about whether some deal is good or not. People of course have less money to play with because of the tax, but it does not stop them from playing well with it. They will still seek out the best possible exchanges and no opportunities for exchange will go unexploited. In practice, the head tax has rarely been used, and when it has been, it has almost invariably led to popular revolt. We shall not discuss it further here.

The non-linearity of deadweight loss

AN EFFICIENT TAX system should minimize deadweight losses for each dollar of revenue the government collects. The premise here is that the deadweight loss from a dollar of tax depends on some feature of the tax that is within government's control. Formula One race car designers shape their car frames to minimize drag and turbulence from air currents. Similarly, government can "shape" taxes to minimize their drag on the economy.

The drag in question arises from a property of deadweight loss known as non-linearity. Non-linearity is a concept imported from mathematics. Applied to taxation it states that each unit increase in tax creates a more than proportional increase in the deadweight loss. It is solely because of this non-linearity that the discussion of efficient taxes has any meaning. Let us first try to understand what non-linearity means and then we will see how so many prescriptions for government radiate from this property of deadweight losses.

Non-linearity is an important topic in physics and biology where it is the idea that drives chaos theory and theories about the origins of order in the universe. Closer to home, non-linearity is well understood by anyone who has fretted about the costs of driving a car. Doubling one's speed more than doubles the use of gasoline. Doubling the speed again more than doubles the use of gasoline above the previous increase. People who like to drive fast have non-linearity to curse for the significant increase in gasoline consumption that comes from accelerating to higher speeds.

Our bodies also feel the effects of non-linearity. Walking slowly up the stairs is far less tiring than walking slightly faster. In all physical endeavours doubling one's performance calls for more than double the effort to achieve that result. From the business world you will no doubt have heard the expression "diminishing returns" to indicate that throwing more resources at a problem brings progressively less impressive results. These shifting results and demands are all members of the family of non-linear effects.

Why should the deadweight loss from a tax be non-linear? The reason is that taxes kill increasingly productive activities for every additional dollar raised. As you tax corporations, at first only the least efficient ones will go out of business. These are the ones with outdated machinery and bad labour relations. Not much is lost by their disappearance. Every subsequent increase of equal increments in the tax knocks out ever more efficient and profitable firms. Each dollar of additional tax becomes a burden that can break the backs of even the most efficient companies. Non-linearity is at play because the first dollar of tax raised costs less than the last dollar when costs are counted in deadweight loss.

The theoretical rule for efficient taxation

ARMED WITH THE concept of non-linearity we are ready to understand why the question of an optimal tax arises solely from non-linear increases in deadweight loss. Consider two different methods of raising a hundred dollars of tax from two people. The government could ask each to pay fifty dollars, or it could place the full burden on one and ask nothing of the other. Non-linearity means that the deadweight loss from a hundred dollar tax paid in equal halves by each of two identical people is less than the loss from having one person pay the entire tax. The reason is that if you tax each person equally, then the deadweight loss from the fiftieth dollar each pays is identical. If one person had to pay the whole sum, the deadweight loss from the first fifty dollars he or she paid would be the same as that felt by the first taxpayer in the case of equal sharing. But the deadweight loss associated with the next fifty dollars he or she paid would be higher per dollar than the highest deadweight loss felt by the second person in the case of equal sharing due to non-linearity. So the sum of deadweight loss for the first fifty and last fifty paid by one person would exceed the sum of the deadweight losses paid by two people each paying fifty dollars.

The Brazilian government learned this lesson to its detriment in the early 2000s when Shell Brazil decided to close several hundreds of its gas stations in reaction to excessively high taxes. The government had felt obliged to target Shell and other high profile producers with high taxes because it was unable to tax independent gas stations that were good at concealing their earnings. The economic consequence of this was that Shell shut down not only inefficient stations that were earning little profit, but was driven also to shut down ordinarily high-yielding stations that were performing an important service to the public. Had the tax been evenly divided among Shell and the independents, then certainly inefficient independent stations would also have closed, but because the burden would have been spread evenly, the lower tax that resulted would have spared Shell from closing its most efficient stations.

The Shell Brazil example illustrates why an efficient tax system is one in which each citizen carries some reasonable fiscal backpack, rather than one that piles spine-bending loads on just a few. This is the principle of efficient taxation at its simplest. There are deviations, but as we shall see, an even spreading of the load remains at the heart of all recipes for efficient taxation.

The competitive advantage of countries that tax efficiently

ECONOMISTS HAVE WORKED diligently to devise efficient systems of taxation because such systems allow government to invest in public goods at the lowest possible deadweight cost. Public goods such as infrastructure (like bridges and roads) are vital to economic development. We can appreciate the importance of public goods purchased through efficient tax systems by looking at poor countries. They offer an extreme example of the manner in which inefficient tax systems can put a brake on development.

One of the almost universal features of poor countries is that they suffer from high rates of tax evasion compared to rich countries. A high rate of evasion means that these governments have relatively few evident targets upon which they can levy taxes. Foreign corporations wishing to exploit natural resources for a fee are often the only reliable source of government revenue. In extreme cases, taxes take the form of stolen lives. People either have their time and effort stolen by forced military service where the government "rents" them out as labourers, or it sets them directly to building roads or working in mines.

As we saw in the previous section, when you focus taxes disproportionately on a narrow segment of the economy, excessive deadweight losses result. In the case of poor countries, corporations stop investing, young men stop working and defect to fight for rebel groups, and the consumer hides his or her savings under the bed. The national income that is lost when foreign companies are discouraged from investing and the mayhem created by private militias are among the deadweight losses produced by these inefficient systems of taxation.

The logic behind foreign aid is that it should enable poor countries to overcome the tyranny of high deadweight losses per dollar of tax levied. In rich countries, most people pay taxes without question. Their deadweight loss from taxation is lower than that of poor countries because the burden is more evenly spread. By lending money to poor countries, rich countries are lending their ability to generate funds at low deadweight losses. The road that would cost a poor country a million dollars in cash plus another million in deadweight losses that would come from raising the money through taxes will cost it a million plus perhaps a hundred thousand dollars in interest if borrowed from a rich country. The theory is that once it has built its infrastructure and protected its property rights, the poor country will have developed a broad tax base from which it can repay its loans at a now reduced domestic deadweight loss.

Getting everyone to pay their taxes is not a question of fairness for poor countries. It is a question of survival and is one part of the puzzle to attaining prosperity. As more people pay the taxes they owe, the burden on those already paying can fall, and the deadweight loss per unit of tax can also fall. One can understand this point best by reading the works of Richard Abel Musgrave, a tireless exponent of efficient taxation in less developed countries.

Refinements to the idea of efficient taxes

THE EXAMPLE OF poor countries suggests that the first step towards efficient taxation is the conquest of tax evasion. Countries that have been successful in taming, if not eliminating evasion, followed a three-pronged approach. First, they developed sophisticated means of measuring the value of property and the incomes people earn. Second, they managed to gradually eliminate legally entrenched evasion, such as official exemptions from tax. Concerning these first two points, economic historian Carlo Cipolla explains in his book *Before the Industrial Revolution* that the

> preindustrial state did not have at its disposal the techniques and the means of investigation available to the industrial state... Moreover, the nobles and the clergy normally enjoyed fiscal immunity... In the course of time both the Church and the nobility lost ground in their effort to evade taxes... Still, over most of Europe for most of time fiscal privileges were a reality that created delays, reduced receipts, and complicated the tax raising process. (page 40)

Finally and perhaps most importantly, countries that are now rich managed to convince people that it was in their interests to voluntarily pay taxes. What economists Bruno Frey and his collaborator Benno Torgler have dubbed "tax morale" depends in great part on the public's belief that government is working on their behalf and that the money they are paying for public services is being well spent. Such beliefs are found in countries where government has corruption and inefficiency under control.

One must be aware of this historical context to appreciate that the fundamental principle of efficient taxation, which is to spread the burden evenly, is not one that can be clinically prescribed. It emerges at the confluence of many reinforcing social and technological currents. From the perspective of economics, tax evasion is a source of deadweight losses. From the sociological perspective it is a display by the citizen who evades of profound disrespect for the citizen who pays his or her taxes. Whatever perspective one takes, taming tax evasion remains a vexing struggle.

Countries that had sought to reduce evasion to acceptable levels could then allow themselves to consider refinements to the even spreading of the tax burden. Saying that efficient taxes are spread evenly has some meaning, but is imprecise. The first serious effort at greater precision came from Cambridge mathematician Frank Ramsey in the 1920s. Ramsey was a friend of John Maynard Keynes, Bertrand Russell, and Ludwig Wittgenstein. He was someone who would have joined the pantheon of the world's great minds had he not died at a very young age. Food poisoning claimed his life at the age of 26, but before then, he managed to found the modern theory of optimal taxation. His prescription was to tax all goods at the same rate in some circumstances, and to tax most heavily those goods that did not respond much to changes in price in other circumstances. If you absolutely need to buy cigarettes, then a tax will not discourage you from your purchase. This makes you a promising target for Ramsey tax commissars. Your inflexibility means that the tax will not discourage you from entering into profitable exchanges.

If everyone is similar and works a fixed number of hours, Ramsey suggested it made sense to tax all goods at the same rate. This turns out to be exactly the same thing as a flat or "linear" tax on income. Problems arise with this simple view once we admit that some goods are hard to tax. In such cases, Ramsey's prescription was to tax most heavily goods that people keep consuming even when prices rise steeply. The idea is that in a world where taxes distort relative prices, we want taxes to create the smallest possible disruptions to consumption patterns because any deviation from these patterns will push us further away from the point where all gains from trade are exploited. This rather complicated analysis was just the first wrinkle of many that would appear on the face of efficient tax theory.

In 1957, Richard Lipsey and Kelvin Lancaster came up with a "second-best theory" of government intervention that had applications to efficient taxation. The deadweight loss from a tax in one sector of the economy might be not be so bad if this tax somehow reduced activity in another part of the economy where deadweight losses were high due to another tax. For example, a tax on cigarettes could cause a deadweight loss to smokers, but the resulting decrease in disposable income might cause a reduction in the consumption of highly taxed and harmful alcohols. Further twists in the theory of efficient taxation came with Arnold Harberger's 1964 analysis of the effect of taxes on investment, and with insights by British economists in the 1970s who sought to favour the poor over the rich by attaching "distributional weights" to the deadweight losses from different economic classes.

Efficient taxation theory became like Scheherazade's telescoping stories in the *Arabian Nights*. Some economists felt that the theory had become a baroque, confusing, and ultimately quixotic quest to engineer behaviour on a mass scale through detailed modifications to the tax system. Most economists simply turned their backs on the subject. In the end, even the experts returned to a simpler conception of what efficient taxation should be. Summing up a vast body of research in a survey on taxation, Nobel Prize winning economist Joseph Stiglitz came to the following conclusion

> The suggestion contained in some of the numerical calculations, namely that the overall welfare gains from optimal taxation (using a utilitarian welfare criterion) are small and that the optimal tax structure may be close to linear, indicates that it may not be unreasonable to focus attention on linear tax structures" (page 1038).

A linear tax structure is a flat tax. At the end of the hunt for an efficient tax, economists return to a proportional distribution of taxes amongst all.

The political side of efficient taxation

SIMPLE TAX SYSTEMS based on a broad spreading of the burden make not only good economic sense but also good political sense because their inbuilt simplicity thwarts the efforts of those who would bend the tax system to their advantage. When we allow tax rates to vary from good to good, or between income classes as prescribed by some of the more complex theories about optimal taxation, the effect is akin to a siren blaring out and calling interest groups that are keen on seeing taxes amended in their favour. The staggering complexity of the US income tax code is not due to politicians following the tutelage of Ramsey-minded economics professors who advise subtly, but the consequence of interest groups pushing ceaselessly for changes to the tax code in their favour and of politicians promoting, perhaps unconsciously, class hatred through progressive income taxation.

Europe does not suffer from a similar tax code complexity because most taxes in Europe are simple "flat" taxes, such as sales taxes, and social security levies that do not allow exceptions. US economists became interested in European-style flat taxes in the 1980s when it became clear that the theory of optimal taxation was not just a mechanical template based on demand and supply but also had to be tempered by the theory of interest group pressure. As Ramsey's theory shows, flat taxes may or may not minimize deadweight loss. But the salient advantage of flat taxes is that they are simple.

Simplicity discourages tax accountants and professional lobbyists from trying to get around taxes. This is an important benefit because when smart people divert their efforts from productive pursuits in the sciences, the arts, and construction towards the evasion of taxes, riches are lost. The riches lost by the "brain drain" away from productive pursuits to the pursuit of cutting the government pie by altering the tax code is a deadweight loss that plagues tax systems that open themselves up to complicated amendments.

Regulations as hidden taxes

THE POLITICAL ANGLE to taxation is difficult enough to spy when talking about taxes that are plainly labeled taxes. What about taxes in disguise? That is, what about regulation? Regulations belong in this chapter because they are taxes and spending rolled into one. Take the Lex Roscia Theatralis of 67 BC, which, as I am sure you are aware, reserved fourteen rows in the theatre for members of Rome's equestrian order. These rows represented lost revenues to theatre owners and as such were a form of tax. The law also specified how these rows were to be used. Allocating a resource to a specific use is a form of expense. Politicians may be tempted to allocate a theatre owner's seats instead of taxing the population directly and spending the money openly on those seats. A tax is a visible irritant apt to provoke protest. The burden of a regulation falls on just a few theatre owners whose ability to protest may be feeble.

Regulations are also a way for governments to spend money without having to present accounts to the public or the legislature. Who has heard of a government budget that includes the tax implicit in price controls, regulation of telephony, or worker safety standards? All are taxes and expenditures, but by virtue of being called regulations they pass unnoticed by tax theorists, and unspoken of in discussions of optimal taxation.

If government can get a job done either by taxing or regulating, which "policy instrument" should it choose? The answer could bring new insights to the debate over the minimum wage. The minimum wage is a regulation that forces employers to pay more for workers than they would have to pay for them in a competitive market. The difference between the minimum wage and what the competitive wage would be is the "tax" which the regulation levies on the employer, and at the same time is the "expenditure" devoted to improving the lot of the worker. As a tax, the minimum wage imposes a deadweight loss. Faced with increased labour costs, some employers go out of business, and some workers lose their jobs. A government that wants to avoid this sort of collateral damage could help workers directly by giving them a handout. But this also creates collateral damage because the handout has to be financed by taxes. Government should choose the intervention that produces the desired result at the least deadweight cost.

The choice between handouts and the minimum wage hinges on whether the minimum wage is a precise instrument that can target mainly the poor. The problem with the minimum wage is that it goes not just to the working poor, but to students from well-to-do families who flip burgers for pocket money, and to well-off retirees who work for amusement. It is an imprecise instrument for redistribution because it expands the ranks of beneficiaries to include those who cannot really be considered needy.

If for every hundred dollars of aid to the poor, the minimum wage also gives a hundred dollars to the rich, then its precision is fifty percent. If government can identify the needy with greater than fifty percent precision, then the case for handouts over minimum wages strengthens. The final verdict depends on a comparison of how broadly the tax can be spread over the population and how broadly the minimum wage falls on employers. If tax evasion is under control, then the taxable base becomes the whole economy. Since employers of low wage labour are a subset of the economy, we can conclude that the minimum wage falls on a narrower section of the economy than do handouts financed by direct taxes. Taxes involve almost everyone in financing the state and so allow the burden of government action to be spread evenly. Regulations target a narrow range of businesses as those to be involved in financing. By transferring more money than the tax does and drawing that transfer from a narrow base, the minimum wage generates more deadweight loss than do taxes imposed on a broad base and used to pinpoint aid to the needy. Its imprecision, combined with the narrow base upon which it falls, can make the minimum wage a sloppy and expensive way of helping the poor.

Such is the case for economies in which tax evasion is low and governments can precisely target needy groups. Minimum wages can make sense in countries where governments are neither competent enough to collect taxes nor skilful or honest enough to target aid to those in need. Think of the minimum wage as a means of controlling the price of labour. When you control a price you are doing something similar to taxing or subsidizing, which are the basic activities of government. If government is unable to raise revenues by taxing directly then it may need to control prices in order to mimic what taxes might do. This may explain why edicts to control prices were popular with governments until the mid-19th century. We still see poor countries taking seriously controls on the price of food and wages. Their lack of an efficient tax system forces them into this posture. In rich countries, price controls have almost disappeared. Minimum wages are relics of an earlier time. Today most governments set them so low that their nuisance to market forces is nugatory.

Governments in rich countries have weaned themselves from direct price controls, but they still depend on a type of regulation that resembles the feudal rights granted by kings. These rights arose in the Middle Ages, sometime after the fall of Rome, when governments lost the ability to tax and administer their domains. The king delegated to a knight the right to rule over a fief. In return, knights pledged to fight for the king in war, and in peace to kick back revenues extracted from serfs. Knights also took upon themselves the administration of local justice.

Today we need not look far to discover that in some industries the spirit of feudal systems lingers. This is no more apparent than in the cable television industry. One becomes a cable operator by lobbying government for the right to a monopoly over the distribution of television signals. The monopoly allows the operator to charge a price in excess of that which would prevail in a competitive market. The excess can be considered a tax. In return for the right to levy this tax, government asks the monopolist to subsidize the production of cultural and public service programming that would normally not appear in a competitive market. Here, as in the case of the minimum wage, the question is whether the cable monopolist's levy falls on a sufficiently broad base to be deemed efficient in comparison to a government tax that could be spent to achieve the same results of subsidizing culture.

Telephony is another example of an industry in which government delegates its powers of taxation and expenditure to corporate barons. In return for a monopoly over land lines, the telephone company agrees to install connections in private homes free of charge for the multi-thousand dollar cost of this service. The company recoups its costs by inflating the price of long-distance calling in an exercise known as cross-subsidization, thereby taxing heavy users of long-distance telephone calls. As with the case of cable monopolies, we must ask whether the telephone "tax" falls on too narrow a base, thereby provoking large deadweight losses compared to the losses that would result from taxing the general population and subsidizing local installation of lines from general government revenues. At the height of this form of hidden taxation, corporations in North America were having their own private telephone lines strung between cities to bypass the punitive long-distance rates they faced. Such a diversion of corporate effort from the real business of the company must be considered a significant deadweight loss.

The lesson from these examples is that we must look at regulations in the same way we look at taxes. Does the regulation spread its burden over a broad base? Is the regulation well-targeted? Unless the answer to both these questions is in the affirmative, the validity of regulation as a means of fixing some gap left by market failure must be questioned.

The Buchanan-Brennan conjecture

TO SUMMARIZE THIS chapter, taxes discourage people from investing, consuming, and working. The result is a loss of Pareto efficiency. There is no point in whining about this because we need taxes to finance collective enterprises such as property rights protected by law, and the provision of public goods and the protection of common property. If we can devise taxes that minimally disrupt Pareto efficiency, then we can afford more of the public goods that themselves add to Pareto efficiency. The key insight in devising an efficient tax is to recognize the non-linear nature of deadweight losses from taxation. Non-linearity means that taxes produce deadweight losses that mount exponentially if they are levied upon some narrow group in society. The solution is to find some means of spreading the tax burden in such a way that no one is forced to carry a crushing fiscal backpack. What exactly this means is a question for economic specialists, but opinion is converging on the flat tax as one that may minimize the deadweight loss per dollar of government revenue gained. Such is the meaning of an efficient tax.

The theory of efficient taxation and regulation would be good news for those living in Pareto's Republic if all else remained constant. Yet the world seldom joins us in our conspiracy to keep things just as they are. Increases in efficiency may provoke reactions. Efficient taxation encourages people to demand big government, as Gary Becker and Casey Mulligan showed. With larger government comes the challenge of knowing what people want and informing them of what they are getting. Without such information, bigger government may become a financial cow ready for milking by selfish interest groups.

Nobellist James Buchanan and his colleague Geoffrey Brennan anticipated with dread Becker and Mulligan's findings. Years before, they feared that efficient taxes would seduce citizens into allowing government to grow into a mythical monster they referred to from Hobbes' writings as "Leviathan." Yes, efficient taxes reduce the disruptions to Pareto efficiency that are the by-product of government intervention, but the large government that results will exploit its coercive power in a way that makes it a direct threat to Pareto efficiency.

Up to a point, increasingly efficient taxation will allow government to strengthen its protection of property and the commons. Yet as government grows, it becomes more difficult for the people to understand whether they are getting a good deal for their tax dollars. Politicians and interest groups exploit this gap in voter knowledge to enrich themselves, and government becomes needlessly costly. A tax has attained its optimum level of efficiency at the point where the benefits of efficiency begin to be outweighed by the costs of losing control over our leaders. Even if this style of thinking seems daunting to non-economists, the point Buchanan and Brennan made was simple. Designing a tax system should not only be an exercise in economic science, but also an exercise in political science. So let us explore politics to see how it can be harnessed to serve the purpose of Pareto's Republic.

POLITICS 6

T HE PREVIOUS THREE CHAPTERS OF this book gave a fairly complete tour of the setting in which Pareto efficiency can thrive and the wealth that can result. But something is missing from this tour of Pareto's Republic. So far, I have been talking about government as if it were an impartial force doing the best it can to promote Pareto efficiency in the face of the challenge of the breakdown of property rights. Where does such a beneficent government come from? In the private market we saw that efficient producers emerge from a struggle for survival within the peaceful strictures of the rule of law. Competition allows efficient producers to replace inefficient ones. Who drives government to be efficient?

Government, as we have described it, is an institution with a monopoly on power. It is not an entity you would think would yield easily to being replaced by a more efficient competitor. After all, if you have the army and police behind you, why would you cede your place to an alternate regime that can manage the state better than you can? The monopoly that government retains on power is an important and sometimes determining factor that stops societies from attaining Pareto efficiency.

Yet we have no choice but to concede a monopoly of force to government. Think what it means to have two governments ruling the same domain. That is a recipe for confusion, if not for all-out civil war. The trick to getting a government that acts Pareto-efficiently is to accept that only one government may rule at a time, but it must simulate around it the conditions of peaceful market competition. Somehow we must devise a means by which a government may be replaced peacefully by another government at some reasonable interval. A more subtle simulation of competition is to create a decentralized political system in which people can move to other jurisdictions that may be run differently and offer an alternate model of governance to citizens who are not pleased with the regime under which they are living. "Voting with your feet" is perhaps the strongest method of containing governments that abuse their monopoly over coercion.

The payoff from creating competition in the "political market" is riches. Peaceful political competition attracts rulers who are best suited to providing the most efficient level of public goods and to protecting common property resources. As we saw in the previous three chapters, these are the two functions of government that create a setting in which people can fully explore the potential for creating wealth. Political competition attracts the most productive rulers in the same manner that private competition under the rule of law attracts people into functions and roles best suited to their abilities.

In private markets, rule of law ensures that the ability to get away with bullying and intimidation are not factors in the individual's rise to success. Rule of law strips people of the power to intimidate, leaving them to use only their productive talents to make their way in the world. In the same manner, peaceful political competition does not allow strongmen or women to shoot or intimidate or bribe their way into office. The road to power is then open to people of all political talents. Bill Clinton's rise from poverty to become one of the most highly acclaimed American presidents is an example of what political competition can produce. Conversely, the rise of dictators who preside over stagnation shows that countries ruled by intimidation are missing out on the chance to create riches. Think of the incredibly fertile country of Zimbabwe which is mired in poverty bordering on famine, courtesy of the paralyzing effect its violent ruler has had on any private initiative to exploit the country's fertility. One can imagine a picture of trees with low hanging fruit just above the reach of a populace debilitated by the numbing action of truncheons bouncing off innocent heads.

In his celebrated treatise, *The Rise and Decline of Nations*, Mancur Olson called such unexploited riches "big bills on the pavement," which are there for the taking if a country invests in property rights, curbs tax evasion, and provides public goods. The big bills remain lying there when the peaceful political competition that would allow the best leaders the chance to pick them is stifled. Potholes are the best example of such uncollected riches. One pothole on a city street can produce tens or hundreds of thousands of dollars of damage to cars' suspensions as drivers pass over them with teeth clenched. Yet the pothole would cost little more than a few hundred dollars to fill by city workers. Here is clearly a case where if drivers paid a little more in taxes they could save much more in repair bills and city workers could benefit from the extra demand for their services. The fact that this potential for improvement on the side of consumers and producers of the political service goes unrealized represents a big bill lying on the pavement, almost literally. That bill could be collected by both citizens and government employees if we had a political system that allowed us to pick up these big bills. How to get such a political system, one that can unite voter-consumers with politician-producers in a union that serves the interest of both, is the subject of the present chapter. It will not surprise you to learn that the lessons of Pareto efficiency in private markets can also be our guide in political markets. This is perhaps the most challenging chapter in the book because it brings together in a unified whole various concepts of the private search for efficiency with society's collective search for the right type and size of government.

So a brief road map may help understand how the ideas will flow. The first part of this chapter explains how notions of competition in private markets can be applied to political markets. First, I start with an analogy, then I explain why the analogy is not perfect. People in a group decide differently from the way an individual decides, and when people consume a government product, one size must fit all, unlike in a private market. The consequence is that political markets are innately less able than private markets to tailor production to private needs. In addition to this inevitable feature of political markets, we come upon the problem of politicians trying to block access to power, thereby restricting competition. As a result, there are two immense problems facing societies that wish to have competition in politics. The first problem is that there are natural barriers to satisfying everyone's needs. The second problem is that there are artificial barriers put in place by politicians.

Despite these obstacles, there are two hopes for achieving political competition. The first resides in people's mobility. If you can run away from an abusive government, then you deprive it of your personal wealth. The consequence is that mobility disciplines irresponsible governments by confronting them with the loss of their best and brightest. The second hope lies in the formal institution of democracy.

Neither of these mechanisms for producing political competition is perfect. What is laudable about democratic systems is that despite their lack of perfection, they can put into power people who are generally peaceful. To understand this road map, we must begin by picking apart the concept of competition, be it in private or political markets. Competition is the force that can produce efficient government. Let us see if this claim makes sense.

What is a political market?

IN PRIVATE MARKETS, competition controls both firms and consumers, forcing both parties to reveal their preferences and their costs. One may think a similar force could constrain governments and lead them to provide us with public goods and the protection of the commons at some reasonable "price." It is tempting to see an analogy between a government that provides a service and a private firm that does the same. Let us see whether the analogy can be pushed far enough to tell us what ingredients are needed to get Pareto-efficient government.

"Political" and "market" seem like two words that don't belong in the same phrase. Politics is the realm of rulers, and the market is the business of producers. The phrase "political market" starts to have some meaning if we think of politicians as producers of public goods and voters as consumers who pay a tax "price" for these public goods.

Though it is sometimes hard to believe, we elect politicians to be our servants, not our masters. These servants have a duty that is similar to the duty of producers in a private market. We voter-consumers elect politician-producers to provide good quality government services at a low tax price. In this sense, if we are lucky enough to live in one, a democracy is nothing more than an instrument for controlling the quality and price of the government we receive.

The analogy between private and public markets is not perfect. In private markets, the consumer can choose the precise amount of product to consume and may switch producers if he or she is not happy. In political markets, each voter-consumer must accept the same offering of public goods as everyone else receives, and he or she can only switch politician-producers once every several years, and then only with the backing of other voters. In political markets, choice and consumption are collective pursuits. The power of our analogy is that by allowing us to see that the political market works like an imprecise, unwieldy economic market, we can assess it using the tools of modern economic reasoning, which was our guide in exploring how to get Pareto efficiency in private markets.

The first to apply the tools of economics to politics were Duncan Black, Friedrich Hayek, James Buchanan, Gordon Tullock, Anthony Downs, and Gary Becker. Their efforts, aptly summarized in Dennis Mueller's opus magnum *Public Choice III*, gave rise to what is now known as the field of Public Choice. They identified the problems political markets face in creating the climate of competition needed to bring people the level of public goods they desire. How to get government to give us what we want is an age-old question that goes back to Cicero's *De Officiis* where he wrote that,

> For if each of us proposes to rob or injure one another for our personal gain, then we are clearly going to demolish the link that unites every human being with every other. Just imagine if each of our limbs had its

own consciousness and saw advantage for itself in appropriating the nearest limb's strength! Of course our whole body would inevitably collapse and die. In precisely the same way, a general seizure and appropriation of other people's property would cause the collapse of the human community.

After Cicero, Madison, Montesquieu, and subsequent political thinkers took up the theme of conflict between private and public interest. Each of these thinkers provided some insights, but it took the arrival of Public Choice experts to snap together the pieces of economic and political thinking into a seamless whole. As the pieces clicked, Public Choice produced a simple, clear, revolutionary way of thinking about how private and political markets should work together. This is one of the great intellectual achievements of the 20th century. In a manner that these thinkers could not foresee, their accomplishments formed the basis of a complete science of peace based on Pareto efficiency.

Political competition

OUR UNDERSTANDING OF political competition starts with some words by Evsey Domar, a great teacher of economics. There is perhaps no better an explanation of what competition means than his: "The power exercised by consumers over producers requires no police, no compulsion, and no letters to the editor of *The New York Times*. It works silently, like gravity. All the consumer has to do is not come back to the store, not buy the same product ever again" (page 36). The power Domar is talking about is that over prices. By changing whom they buy from, consumers force greedy producers to either lower their prices or else to go out of business. Competition pushes producers to lower their prices almost to the level of their costs. The same principle applies in labour markets where competition between firms drives up wages to reflect the productivity of workers. This is why economists say that competition is a mechanism for revealing cost and productivity.

It is all well and fine to speak about switching allegiances, but then why do so many people feel stuck in an abusive relationship with one producer? The feeling of being stuck arises in two instances. Either you do not know what your alternatives are, or you are not allowed to move towards those alternatives. Put differently, being able to switch whom you buy from or whom you sell your labour to depends on knowing what choices are open to you and on the freedom to make these choices. This is why throughout history producers who fear the strength of competition have tried to limit information and choice.

This precise way of defining competition and identifying its two main ingredients, information and choice, dispel the fuzzy popular misconceptions of competition as war that are so enshrined in popular culture. Michael Crichton's *Rising Sun* portrayed the commercial rivalry between the US and Japan as a bloody conflict. Crichton might as well have been thinking of Assyrian king Tikulti-Ninurta who boasted that, "I brought about defeat of his armies, his warriors I overthrew. In the midst of that battle my hand captured Kashtilash, the Kassite king. I trod on his royal neck with my feet like a footstool." Clearly Ninurta had a drive to compete, but not one we would wish to promote in those with whom we do business. The type of competition that flows from information and choice is not an assault, but rather a form peaceful negotiation. This is why Pareto-efficient exchanges of private goods between people lead to peace.

The same principle can be put to work in politics. A Pareto-efficient political market is one that allows people to collectively choose the level of public goods and property rights protection that maximizes the potential for Pareto-efficient wealth creation in the private sector. That means getting a government that will spend a hundred dollars to fill the pothole that is destroying wheel bearings, axles, and possibly dental work, worth tens of thousands of dollars. It also means getting a government that focuses on providing public goods at some reasonable tax cost. Competition gives voter-consumers an informed choice between several candidates or parties. Information allows voters to decide which candidates are best able to provide public goods at a reasonable tax price, whereas the ballot, and other means of voting to be discussed later, allows voters to exercise that choice.

Natural barriers to entry in politics

As ALLURING AS the above analogy between the market and political competition may be, getting a Pareto-efficient government is not easy. There are two main reasons why political markets can only ever be a pale imitation of private markets. The first, and perhaps most important reason, is that political markets do not require that everyone be persuaded, as private markets do. Remember that to be Pareto- efficient, an exchange must have a one hundred percent agreement among the parties.

If we apply the same principle to political markets, then it is likely that government will become paralyzed. We need to accept something less than a one hundred percent approval rating, which is why most collective choice takes place by majority rule. The challenge this poses to getting Pareto-efficient government is that sometimes a majority will use its coercive power not to promote the purchase of public goods, but rather to exploit minorities through large-scale government redistribution of private resources. We will see later in this chapter that as a consequence, no system of collective choice can work unless property rights are secure from such depredations.

The second reason for being careful about making the analogy between private and public markets is that the challenges to acquiring information and exercising choice differ considerably between private and public settings. Public Choice scholar Charles Rowley has clarified the nature of the challenge we face in finding a government that promotes Pareto efficiency. In a defining essay on this question, he wrote that if "problems of monopoly, externalities, public goods, and bounded rationality afflicted private markets; they simply ravaged political markets that confronted individuals with massive indivisibilities and severely limited exit options" (page 10). This is a rough sentence to understand so let us break it down into its components.

By indivisibilities, Rowley means that government produces goods such as health care or education in giant packets that cannot be tailored to any one individual's needs, the way some private goods may be tailored. This sort of indivisibility makes it difficult for individuals to express their needs as they would when they pay directly for some private good or service. Without such signals from voter-consumers, politician-producers are working in an environment of limited information.

By problems of monopoly Rowley is saying that when a producer of a private good becomes the sole supplier, consumers suffer, but they can limit their pain by cutting back on their consumption or finding substitutes. However, when faced with a government that has a monopoly on coercion, voters have no substitutes that they can immediately seek out. One must wait years until the next election or the next revolution comes along.

By externalities Rowley is thinking of common property of a very specific sort. We are used to thinking of virgin forests and shoals teeming with fish as common properties open to devastation by unbridled economic exploitation. Rowley carries this image over to government where treasuries can be thought of as a form of common fiscal property that can be ravaged on a massive scale by battles between interest groups.

Taken together these points suggest that the problems of commercial markets mutate into monstrosities once we move to political markets. This is due to the indivisible nature of what government produces and the potentially rivalrous means by which society determines that level of production. The challenge Rowley lays down is how to fix an institution that on its own has deficiencies (markets) with an institution that has potentially even greater deficiencies (government).

In the *Review of Economic Literature,* economist James Rauch phlegmatically summarized the stunted condition of current knowledge concerning the Rowley challenge: "consensus is lacking on exactly how property rights are secured by a given set of institutions" (page 480). Development expert Avinash Dixit adds to the gloomy mood surrounding the search for Pareto-efficient government by suggesting that "processes of creating the institutions and the apparatus of state law, and of improving them to the point where they function well, are slow and costly" (page 4).

What Rowley and others are describing are the so-called natural barriers to achieving competitive politics. They are called "natural" because in a sense we must grin and bear them. That is simply the nature of the political beast. Yet there are also barriers that we need not be so sanguine about because it is we who create them. They are artificial because they can be overcome when people agree to make the political system more open. To understand this distinction, a brief summing up could help.

Artificial barriers to entry

To SUMMARIZE THE chapter so far, competition is a broad principle that can be applied both to private and political markets. In private markets, competition forces people to reveal their preferences for consumption and their abilities to produce. This revelation of information creates a balanced form of social accounting called Pareto efficiency.

When applied to politics, competition gives voter-consumers information and choice about their leaders, which these voters then use to choose leaders who will provide the Pareto-efficient level of public services. The problem with this analogy between private and public competition lies in the fundamental difference between collective goods and private goods, as well as in the difference between how choices are arrived at collectively and privately. As if these inherent challenges to getting competitive government were not daunting enough, there is also a list of challenges we create for ourselves. This is the subject to which we now turn.

Economists use the term "barriers to entry" to describe anything that blocks consumers from becoming informed about and choosing new alternatives. In 1958, in one of the first economic analyses of democracy, Gary Becker wrote that, "In an ideal political democracy competition is free in the sense that no appreciable costs or artificial barriers prevent an individual from running for office, and from putting a platform before the electorate" (page 106). Becker was speaking of politicians, but his idea applies equally well to individuals or groups seeking to influence policy or election outcomes. Artificial barriers to entry do not come about by accident, but rather by the efforts of politicians to protect their positions of power. People in office sometimes change the rules of the political game to make it difficult for new candidates and parties to put their ideas before the public. Public Choice scholars Burton Abrams and Russell Settle explained that this happens because

> Rational, self-interested individuals, groups, or industries seek regulation as a means of serving their own private interests... When regulation has the potential for directly affecting the legislators themselves (e.g., political campaign regulations), the economic approach suggests that the regulation would be designed to serve the legislators' interest rather than some vaguely defined public interest. (page 274)

Examples of such barriers are numerous. Think of the government subsidies that established parties vote themselves, or of the manner in which those in power redefine the borders of electoral districts, so-called gerrymandering, in order to secure a majority. I have written in detail about such barriers and you may find reference to them in an article of mine I cite in the bibliography, but there is no need to further catalogue those barriers here.

What we need to appreciate is that artificial barriers are costly and pernicious. They restrict information and choice, which in turn restricts political competition, which in turn raises the tax price of public goods. They do so in ways that are hard to detect. The causal chain is long and so it is difficult for voters to identify what ails them. Just as some successful parasites in nature do not drain their host too quickly for fear of being noticed, so it is with artificial barriers to entry into politics.

Solution #1 for what ails political competition: mobility

WE CAN ACKNOWLEDGE the difficulties in getting political competition that Rowley and Becker catalogue without inertly capitulating in our search for some solution to the problem. There is a substantial body of research in history, economics, and politics suggesting that two very powerful forces can come to the rescue of political competition. The first of these forces is mobility. The second is democracy. Let us examine each in turn to see how they can help to create governments that respect and seek to enable the Pareto-efficient functioning of society.

Long before scholars began to consider democracy and voting at the ballot box to be the pinnacle of societies that had managed to get their governments under control, people were voting with their feet by fleeing the abuse of harsh rulers. Mobility was always, and remains, one of the key ingredients for promoting political competition. We can appreciate this by considering the inverse proposition: anything that blocks the ability of citizens to move from one government jurisdiction to another, temporarily or permanently or simply for the purposes of travel, limits the availability of political information and choice. In the extreme, an inability to explore what different governments in different places have to offer can be considered a form of captivity.

Captivity is the subject of historian William McNeill's celebrated book, *The Rise of the West*. In it, he suggests that Europe rose to world dominance two hundred years ago because its people became mobile. Mobility allowed both human and physical capital to flee oppression and seek out regimes that favoured them. Talented and rich Europeans found safe haven in countries such as Holland and England that protected property and the person. France and Germany had no option but to follow the English and Dutch examples, or perish from a brain drain and the flight of capital. Carlo Cipolla lists detailed examples of European countries that tried to influence the flow of labour to their advantage. He cites the case of Venice, which forbade caulkers from emigrating, or France, which encouraged master steelworkers to visit, and when that did not work, resorted to kidnapping them at the prompting of Finance Minister Colbert. McNeill concludes that instead of growing, Europe would have stagnated had one empire managed to gain control and impose its will on a captive people, as was the case in China.

Recently, scholars with access to detailed modern data have been able to give statistical support to McNeill's historical analysis and have refined our understanding of the benefits of mobility. Most of this evidence comes from the United States and some focuses on competition between school districts. Student performance is intensively measured in the social sciences and so provides a ready indication of how public schools perform. One finding of these studies, as summarized in a paper by Michael Marlow, is that high performing school districts have a "spill-over" effect on their neighbours. One mechanism that forces underperforming districts to match their better performing rivals is the migration of parents and the loss of tax base that results.

Other research considers the entire United States as a laboratory for policy, with each state serving as a test tube. Political scientist William Barry discovered that states are forced to compete with each other for lottery customers; if the terms of the lottery in one state are poor, citizens of that state will cross to the neighbouring state to shop for tickets where their odds of winning are better. The pressure that people exert on government by voting with their feet is in part responsible for what social scientists call "policy diffusion." In the US, successful sub-federal government policies make their way, or "diffuse," across county and state borders. Information about the effects of those policies encourages neighbouring citizens to lobby for change, and if change isn't forthcoming, to threaten that they will move away from the control of inept governments.

The pattern of diffusion of government services is similar to that for private goods. At first, adoption is slow and mainly the act of a few risk-taking politicians. As the benefits become obvious, the risks of adoption fall and other areas hurry to imitate the pioneers. In this way mobility spreads information, expands choice, and puts pressure on government to offer its services at competitive tax prices.

"Voting with your feet" is perhaps the most fundamental way for people to control the costs of government. It is likely the fount from which springs democracy, as most people understand it. To vote with one's feet, one need not register with an election commission, nor wait for a pre-determined election period to run its course, nor worry about the constitutional validity of the electoral outcome. All one need do is move to put competitive pressure on politicians. The most direct evidence for the fact that rulers fear their subjects voting with their feet lies in their efforts to either keep people in place or to render useless their migrations. Absolute rulers favoured the direct approach of tying people to the land. The late Roman Empire forbade citizens to leave their provinces. Medieval knights ensured themselves a cheap supply of labour by imposing serfdom. The Soviets and their satellites took this concept to unimagined lengths by building a system of fortifications called the Iron Curtain inside of which, for the first time in history, weapons pointed not outward at the enemy, but inward at the population.

Variants on these forms of imprisonment persist in some poor countries, but today's rulers prefer a more subtle approach to the challenge of mobility. Voting with one's feet becomes futile when government finances are concentrated at the highest level of government. There is no point in moving from one municipality to the next, or in crossing regional borders, if all decisions about spending emanate from the nation's capital. Voting with one's feet only works when the tax dollar follows the taxpayer.

Of course, voters may still vote with their feet by moving to other countries, but trans-border brotherhoods of politicians have found ways to defend themselves against this type of competitive threat. In the European Union, member states banded together to impose similar tax rates and regulations across the Eurozone, leaving citizens with nowhere to shop for cheap government. What politicians of the union call tax "harmony," and regulatory "rationalization," is an attempt to impose a uniformity of government from which escape is difficult. The effort the European Union has devoted to homogenizing taxes and regulations stands in contrast to the almost complete indifference the union has shown to regulating the formal democratic institutions of member states.

Democratic institutions that foster information and choice are of little concern to politicians once they have managed to insulate themselves from competition by continent-wide agreements that limit the reform of taxes and regulations. That the power of democratic institutions depends in part on the structure of government finances and regulations is a point seldom emphasized in textbooks or spoken of in public debate.

Czech president Vaclav Klaus was the only European leader to warn of the danger that the centralization of authority posed to national democracies. His prophecies came true in 2010 when European fiscal rules took precedence over local democratic institutions in a manner that led Greeks to riot. The issue in question was the value of the euro, which is tied to the fiscal balance of each member nation. After years of pretense, the Greek government admitted its debt was close to twice the value of its GDP. Instead of dealing with this problem by submitting to the will of electors, the government was bound by its membership in the EU to return to fiscal balance. The central character of the European currency made nonsense of the ability of Greek voters to influence their government.

Solution #2 for what ails political competition: democracy

POLITICAL COMPETITION IS a concept. Democracy is but one instrument for putting that concept into practice. This is why the present chapter kicked off with a discussion of competition, and why now it is proceeding down the list of means by which to attain it. The first instrument discussed was mobility, or so-called "voting with your feet." Now we turn our attention to democracy and the questions of what benefit it brings and how to get it.

It is impossible to escape the image of democracy as people voting either for representatives, or casting their ballots directly for some law, as they might in a referendum. This is a functional image because it is reflected in many of the variants of democracy we see in action and because it helps us sidestep the need to overdefine democracy. There is no need. Everyone knows it when they see it and it does not take an intellectual to point out the original from the fake. All variants of what people think of as democracy share the feature that they try to impose competition on politicians by giving citizens an orderly means of either removing leaders from office or bypassing these leaders entirely through a referendum.

This, at least, is what one hopes. Yet as in the case of voting with one's feet, voting at the ballot box may or may not contribute to political competition. We saw that politicians could neuter the efficacy of voting with the feet if they could somehow manage to standardize policies across national or governmental borders, thereby rendering the notion of mobility meaningless. The same problem of inefficacy can plague democracy. More than half the world's countries have "paper democracies," which are well summarized by the Roman magistrate Licinius Macer. Over two thousand years ago, he told his people that "you have been stripped of every privilege your forefathers left you except your ballots, and by them, you who once chose your defenders now choose your masters." In today's world there are dozens of countries that hold similarly meaningless ballots, and even in countries with strong democratic traditions, such as those in Europe, political scientists are talking about a "democratic deficit" emerging as the feeling grows in voters that they are unable to influence policy.

The lesson is that the institutions of democracy, such as voting and election campaigns, do not by themselves produce political competition. Some added ingredient is needed. The clue to what that ingredient needs to be lies in a remarkable coincidence: we observe no examples of real democracy without property rights being present. Robert Heilbroner wrote in *Twenty-first Century Capitalism* that, "democratic liberties have not yet appeared, except fleetingly, in any nation that has declared itself to be fundamentally anticapitalist" (page 69).

This does not mean that property rights inevitably lead to democracy, but rather, that democracy cannot function without them. Property rights are a necessary, but not a sufficient condition for democracy to emerge. Economist Dan Usher explored this point at length in his landmark book, *The Economic Prerequisites to Democracy*. He warned that a majority winning power at the ballot box by orderly and peaceful means can be just as rapacious and vengeful as any conquering army. Something more than mere balloting is needed to prevent whoever wins at the box from using the coercive power of government to exploit groups who lost the election. To become something more than an instrument for large scale theft, a democracy must exist alongside what Usher described as a fair, inviolable "system of division." People must trust they will be able to divide resources under rules that are equitable and stable and that these rules will resist the comings and goings of governments and popular whims. In principle, many such systems may exist, but in practice, only a system of property rights, protected by rule of law, has proved itself capable of shielding people from the potential excesses of democracy, while restricting government towards questions of public goods and tragedies of the commons.

The dangers of democracy without some background system of restraint were well understood by Voltaire in 18th century France when he equated mass rule with mob rule. They are acutely understood today in Iraq, which has reacted badly to the American attempt at a democratic graft. Sunni Muslims, who are a minority, rightly fear that elections will favour Shiite Muslims, and that this group will limit Sunni access to the mineral wealth of Iraq. The fear arises because petroleum is in government hands, and is there for the taking by whoever controls government.

Sentiments in China are similarly inclined. While tragic, the massacre at Tiananmen Square in 1989 may have been an attempt by the government of China to stop an even more cataclysmic scenario: the eruption of civil war. Democracy could not have come to China in 1989 because property rights had not yet fully arrived. Once China establishes these rights in some stable form we may well see democracy emerge peacefully, as it did in South Korea, Taiwan, and Singapore, which all laid a firm base of property rights before embarking on democratic experiments.

The above ruminations on the preconditions for democracy may seem relevant only to developing countries, but they also hold a lesson for rich countries that have grown smug in the belief that they represent the pinnacle of this institution. Countries that won their democracy long ago, and benefited from it over generations, now face its slow erosion. In a brilliant survey of government growth since the 1870s, Vito Tanzi and Ludger Schuknecht showed not only that governments grew from ten to fifty percent of national income in a one hundred year span, but also that most of government spending by the end of the 20th century was devoted to redistributing money rather than spending that money on building bridges and funding other forms of infrastructure.

This growth in the redistributive function of government is alarming. As a government grows in its power to redistribute resources, it also attracts so-called "rent-seekers," who use democracy as a means to plunder the collective wealth stored in the treasury, much as poachers plunder natural forest preserves.

Ordinarily people think of redistribution as a benign function which governments fulfill in order to help the needy. Yet redistribution is a much broader activity than this notion allows and may have a sinister aspect when the giving goes to people or groups who are not needy but simply powerful and greedy. To block these rent-seekers, modern democracies have had to become less democratic. Constitutional courts are busier than ever and we hear a great many complaints about "court-made law."

Yet what else could we expect? As the pot of money upon which they sit grows, governments become reluctant to make new laws that could further influence the distribution of income in society. Supreme Courts, which can act like small dictatorships, then get burdened with the duty to resolve questions that are simply too divisive to be discussed democratically. The lesson is that the more a society socializes property, the greater is the need for a government that limits conflict between groups by putting strict limits on collective decision making. This explains why "social democracy" is a contradiction in terms. The more socialism you have, the less democracy you can afford. Europe is deep in the dilemma of how to reconcile big government with popular demands for a say in that government. North America still has what might be called vibrant democracy, but that may change if government there continues to bloat.

The two good things about democracy

IF THE ECONOMIC prerequisites are sufficient to produce a democracy in which people can focus on deciding issues of public good rather than in using government as a means to rob each other, then two good things follow. The first good thing about such a democracy is that it produces leaders who are sensitive to the public's needs and who can satisfy these needs competently. The second reason is that democracy imposes upon leaders certain restraints and incentives that also drive them towards satisfying the public's need for public goods and the protection of common property resources.

With reference to the first benefit of democracy, what does it mean to produce a leader sensitive to public needs? Economists are coming to believe that the first order of any business, be it private or government, is to get the right people into the right places. This may sound like a truism, but it is actually one side of a fine distinction. The right people are those who do the right thing, no matter what temptations they may face. The other side of the distinction is that no matter who is in place, it helps if that person has incentives, such as punishments and rewards that encourage him or her to act in the interests of the business. So basically, two things determine whether people behave according to some norm: their inner voice telling them what to do and the outer incentives they face.

A story can make the distinction clear. After WWII, Czechoslovakia became a communist country. The incentives communism offered its people to work were contradictory and usually insufficient to produce the required motivation. But people did work for many years, because that is what they had been trained to do in pre-communist regimes. The "right" people were in place. And that is what mattered most for enabling the communist regime to function in its first few decades. Eventually, though, the right people retired and the people who took their places were those raised in a society without any clear laws or property rights. This was the death-knell of communism. After the fall of communism in 1989, Czechoslovakia found itself a country of cynical shirkers whose caustic outlook on work had been shaped by generations of living in a country where there was no connection between effort and reward. Yet even these shirkers responded to the re-introduction of property rights, which had the immediate and electrifying effect of getting people to respond to basic market incentives. Soon long lines at grocery stores disappeared and food and clothing started to be in more plentiful supply. However, to advance beyond this initial stage of development, a second revolution was needed to get the right people in the right places so that big projects such as shopping malls, hospitals, airports, and banks could be established. What Czechoslovakia (and eventually the Czech and Slovak Republics into which they split) needed was a mechanism by which people best suited to business could rise into positions of responsibility.

What has any of this to do with democracy? If we have a democracy based on property rights, then public office is not the road to personal riches. Property rights are secure. All that government can do is to seek the public good. It can do nothing else because the private pie is protected by law from being cut up through government interventions. Personal glory and a sense of working for the public are the only rewards one can expect in such a system. This reward structure draws in people who have a peaceful mindset and whose goals rise above the material. True democracy is based on property rights, which in turn are an implementation of the peaceful dispute resolution mechanism underlying Pareto efficiency. Taken from the inverse perspective, Pareto efficiency as a principle of peace percolates up from property rights to the manner in which societies govern themselves, a manner that invites as its highest exponents men and women steeped in a belief that peace should reign.

Here, then, is why democracy can be seen as arising from and propagating a civilizing tendency. True democracy weeds out individuals with barbaric leanings and produces leaders steeped in civility. These, in turn, promote better property rights and further enhancements in democracy. It is not popular these days to make such stark distinctions, but the task of describing Pareto's Republic is not a popularity contest. It is based on the alarm now being raised in economics over the importance of institutional mechanisms that determine how people use and develop their talents.

The alarm was raised as early as in 1993 by economists Andrei Schleiffer, Kevin Murphy and Robert Vishny. They showed how societies can spiral into ruin when a brain-drain pulls people out of productive activities in the private sector towards predatory activities at the helm of government. They argued that predatory activities may become more profitable as the number of predators increases. Robbers in small bands are easily caught. As the size of the band increases, the risks fall and the expected gains rise. Also, as predation increases, victims hire some predators to ward off others. Predators in this case are like the unscrupulous doctor who gives his patient drugs that sicken him so that he returns for further treatment. The transfer of talents from productive to predatory activities may accelerate to such a point that society disintegrates into a chaos of warring groups. Friedrich Engels sounded an earlier, similar warning. While discussing the outcome of contests between multitudes for booty, he predicted such conflicts could end in "famine, pestilence, and the general barbarization of both armies and people." Democracy spares us from this apocalyptic scenario by elevating into power people who specialize in providing peace.

Even if the type of people who go into politics are not of the most benevolent disposition, democracy has a secondary advantage, which is to provide leaders, be they good or bad, with an incentive to behave efficiently. As we learned earlier in this chapter, political competition controls the tax price people pay for their chosen level of government services. Competition achieves this by providing voter-consumers with a choice of potential leaders and with information about them. Voter information and choice constrains the ability of politicians to behave inefficiently or corruptly. Democracy is one means of getting this competition. Of course we may complain that we feel stuck with the need to trust our leaders with most decisions. We blame democracy for being a popularity contest, focusing on personalities rather than issues, but that may be an efficient response to the complexity of the tasks that government faces, and an admission that the right person in the right place may be more important than any incentives that person faces.

While the debate on the importance of incentives versus personalities continues, what should be clear by this point is that this debate's most fruitful lesson is that collective decision-making procedures should be called upon sparingly. To reduce collective choice, fraught as it is with non-competitive potential, we should be alert to divesting government of any activity which no longer calls for collective management. Government should be on a constant state of alert for the means by which it can render itself less relevant.

The end of politics

THE PROBLEM WITH democracy or any other system of providing competitive politics is that government is a recalcitrant subject. Unlike a cell phone or a pizza, you cannot consume government services in manageable slices. Your consumption of government comes as a fixed bundle of services. Your willingness to pay plays no direct role in your consumption. Nor does the politician's compensation depend on whether he or she satisfied you directly. When a consumer's willingness to pay becomes muted, and a producer's reward for good service is unclear, then it becomes difficult to coordinate the supply of government services with the demand for them.

Elections try to balance popular needs with government resources, but no one pretends the correspondence is perfect or that everyone is as tightly satisfied as they are in the market for private goods. Researchers try to find the means by which demand and supply for collectively consumed goods can be balanced, but in my view they are fighting a rear-guard action. Democracy can put peaceful people into office. That is its enduring benefit. But then it stumbles in fulfilling the more refined function of providing some Pareto-efficient level of public goods, such as might be called for with Samuelson's rule.

This shortcoming of democracy should not be a paralyzing concern. Democracy helps us scoop up most of the big bills lying on the pavement. We need government to build public infrastructure and protect property rights. Here is where the biggest stash of bills is to be found. Democracy and other schemes for political competition put into power leaders who are adept at helping society pick up most, but not all, of these bills, regardless of what momentary political incentives they may face.

Societies based on dictatorship, or some other such arbitrarily violent form of rule, are geared towards being governed by violent individuals. These predators have a diminished sense of where the big bills lie because they either do not care or are unable to pick them up. The problem with non-democratic societies is one of personality. You cannot separate the violence from the office. The signal contribution of democracy is to allow people to rise to power without reference to violent tendencies.

What should trouble us is when those in power try to erect barriers to the entry of competitors with new ideas and attitudes. Barriers to entry are a never-ending challenge to democracy, as they are to private markets where dominant firms are forever trying to bar new competitors so as to entrench their monopoly positions. The difference, though, is that in commerce, firms cannot use coercion to help them, whereas coercion is government's distinguishing feature.

Democracy and the rules under which government should work are a bit of a mystery to most researchers. What is emerging with some certainty is that if you are going to have a Pareto-efficient society, which at its root is based on a principle of peaceful reconciliation between individuals, then this principle of peace needs to carry over to the government that rules them. Democracy playing out in a society where property is protected under the rule of law is the best bet for such a peaceful arrangement.

FUTURE   7

A LLOW ME TO SUMMARIZE THIS book in one paragraph. Conflicts inevitably occur over the way physical and human resources are to be used. We can never eliminate antagonisms or animosities between people. These will inevitably arise over questions of resource use. Yet we may be able to channel violent inclinations into peaceful and even productive ways of resolving disputes.

One means of channelling these inclinations is to give people property rights protected by the rule of law. With these in place, every disagreement over the use of property is resolved in such a manner that no one is made worse off and at least one person will be made better off. Any such exchange is called Pareto improving. Once people have exhausted all the Pareto improvements possible, they have attained a state of Pareto efficiency. This "peace of Pareto" is superior to other forms of imposed peace, such as central control, because it balances what people owe each other in a more precise and humane manner, one that leads invariably to prosperity. Yet it is impossible to allocate all resources using property rights because sometimes these rights simply cannot be created or established or determined. When property rights are absent, markets fail to correctly balance social accounts; government may step in to correct the imbalance, as it may in the case of public goods and common property resources. The problem then becomes one of ensuring that government, to whom we entrust a monopoly, if even temporary, over coercion, does not abuse its powers to charge a non-competitive "tax price" for doing its duty of plugging the gaps left by incomplete private property rights. More critically, government must be prevented from acting in a short-sighted manner due to the political market's problem of establishing competitive property rights over government power.

This cursory summary of the present book is not a master plan for creating Pareto's Republic. If anything, it should be clear from this book that societies do not follow scholarly guidelines for self-improvement. Yet I do not subscribe to the school of thought that sees society as some mysterious entity proceeding rudderless on its own towards undefined ends. And I see as eccentric the view put forth by Nobel Prize winning economist George Stigler, that if commercial markets could be trusted to behave efficiently, why not believe that political "markets" would also be efficient, and so why seek to change them? In his view, an efficient political market shares with economic markets the feature that every decision that takes place is such that no one could further benefit without someone else getting hurt. Stigler does not distinguish between democracy and a dictatorship. He posits that both systems consist of interest groups vying for control of government resources. These groups use politicians as their agents to broker deals on how government should intervene. Deals will continue to be negotiated by the political go-betweens until at least one interest group sees no benefit to participating. In his essay, *Law or Economics?* Stigler wrote that "every durable social institution or practice is efficient, or it would not persist over time," a line which might have got a chuckle or two out of inmates huddled around the campfire of some gulag or concentration camp, as they learned that their captivity was a manifestation of efficiency.

What Stigler neglected to explore was that efficiency does not come about by itself. Someone has to make systems efficient. That someone could be you, convincing friends that the system has to change and adjust to become more efficient, and they in turn pass the message on. That someone could be the academic who puts in comprehensible form the message that there are opportunities for creating property rights and public goods that go unexploited so that there are "big bills lying on the pavement" for us to take, if only our political system were to change. What this means is that something is blocking people from making deals that could be mutually profitable. It takes effort to spot and then pick up the big bills. They are not simply lying meretriciously on the pavement. Yet with the proper understanding of the importance of property rights and of competition in democracy, and at the base of things a willingness to follow a peaceful means of resolving our differences over the use of resources, we may well scoop them up. After a savage war with their northern brethren, South Koreans decided to become a peaceful people and to express that peace first through commerce, and then through the ensuing democracy. The move to democracy was not accomplished by a revolution of arms, but by an evolution of faith and understanding. The insights of scholars who brought to light the ingredients of competitive markets and competitive politics were a crucial part of that understanding, as they were in Chile's transition first from socialism to property rights in the 1970s, and then from dictatorship to democracy in the 1980s.

Still, there are no guarantees that simply by knowing the ingredients of Pareto efficiency a society can attain that state. There are two challenges to attaining and then maintaining Pareto's Republic. The first and greatest challenge is that of overcoming prejudices and group hatreds. These are fundamentally inimical to any form of productive peace. When antagonisms are too powerful in the very specific sense that I will describe below, property rights or democracy become overwhelmed by the demands upon them to funnel aggression into productive pursuits. The second challenge is more ongoing. It is to fight at every instance the tendency of governments to absorb resources and place them under public control. This is not the cry of the libertarian or neo-conservative, but rather a concern that arises from ongoing research into the dangers of creating common property. Here are my reasons for selecting these two as the most pressing challenges.

Insuperable antagonisms

THE PEACE OF Pareto's Republic is not to be found everywhere. In fact, few countries have managed to even come close to fulfilling the ideals I have outlined here. No one can identify all the barriers to attaining a Pareto-efficient society, but societies too riven with internal hatreds between groups will not be able to explore mechanisms for obtaining peace between individuals. As economist and peace researcher Syed Mansoob Murshed writes,

> The difference between aspirations and reality during a period when general material conditions are improving may induce disadvantaged individuals to revolt. This, however, is more likely to take the shape of organised group conflict when individual and group grievances merge, simply because collective action is easier. (page 2)

This is one example of a more general problem that economists describe as "the non-separability of preferences from production." Less technically, this means that if two groups of people hate each other sufficiently, they will indulge their "tastes" for hatred and fail to come to a deal that would financially profit both sides. Shakespeare provides an early illustration of this point. The Montagues and Capulets could have very profitably married their children to each other, but because of an ancient family hatred, they lost the opportunity to join in love and commerce. In *Vom Kriege*, Carl Von Clausewitz wrote of the "primordial passions of people to prolong war, ignore authority, and escalate conflict" against what appeared to be their best interests.

Labour market economists have understood the danger of non-separability of preferences and production since Gary Becker's ground-breaking work on the economics of discrimination in the 1950s. Competition is powerless to weed out those who link emotion to commerce if all share the same emotion. Racial and gender discrimination in the labour market can last generations if a critical number of employers share the same hatred of targeted groups. Only if some employers care more about their bottom line than about categorizing workers can discrimination be eradicated. Employers who put profits above hatred can draw skilled workers from the discriminated class away from their bigoted competitors and so drive those competitors out of the market.

Unfortunately, the same sort of competitive mechanism works poorly in politics because you cannot drive a socially accepted group out of the "political market" the way you can drive a company out of the commercial market. A Laundromat that discriminates against minorities may have to fold up because its competitor is willing to hire minorities at wages commensurate with their productivity. The failed Laundromat operator exits the market and perhaps becomes a bus driver or a reporter. In contrast, white supremacists cannot be driven out of politics because there is no mechanism for making them leave, similar to the private market mechanism of profit and bankruptcy. This is why Pareto efficiency stands little chance in a society of massed hatreds. It is only a mechanism of dispute resolution in a setting where animosity is individualized, and in consequence can be marginalized through competition for property rights.

Alexis de Tocqueville described these sociological challenges more elegantly in his *Letters from America*, in which he said of American society that, "…the more I see of this land, the more convinced I am of this truth, that there are virtually no political institutions radically good or bad in themselves and that everything depends on the physical conditions and social state of the people to whom they are applied." Thomas Malthus echoed this sentiment in the tenth chapter of the first edition of his book, *An Essay on the Principle of Population,* where he wrote, "But the truth is, that though human institutions appear to be the obvious and obtrusive causes of much mischief to mankind; yet, in reality, they are light and superficial, they are mere feathers that float on the surface, in comparison with those deeper seated causes of impurity that corrupt the springs, and render turbid the whole stream of human life."

Societies can, and do, slowly escape from turbid depths of group hatred, and perhaps the slow introduction of property rights has something to do with that. This is the sociological dimension of Pareto efficiency which is only now coming to be appreciated by scholars. The example of the Dutch illustrates this point. The history of Holland can be seen as the quest to expand its landmass by building dikes around ocean flats and pumping away the sea water. The complexities of dike management forced different groups of landowners to negotiate with each other for the rights to drain water from one property to another on its final destination to the ocean. Paradoxically, the "selfish" institution of property led to extended negotiations which forced everyone to compromise and develop a spirit of cooperation. Today the Dutch are among the most "socially conscious" people in the world. No one can say for sure, but perhaps because of their powerful commercial sense and pioneering efforts to create and sustain complex property rights the Dutch were able to combine rapid population growth with a continued sense of community. At around the same time as Holland was developing a decentralized system of property management, China toiled under what historian Karl Wittfogel called "hydraulic tyrants." They dictated how water from the Yangtze should be shared among peasants. This approach to administration retarded China's development of property rights so catastrophically that when Europeans arrived in the 19th century, their armies imposed their wills without contest. They found a divided land in which dozens of cultures and regions were too estranged from one another to join forces and repel invaders. Social solidarity was weak in China without the secure property rights that people needed for settling arguments in a peaceful manner, and by doing so, acquire the habit of peace.

A similar lack of solidarity is evident in many of today's post-communist countries where past leaders intuitively understood that the stability of the regime lay in to dividing one person from another. Many people who moved from the former Soviet Union to America were shocked that Americans cleaned up their dogs' droppings in parks and were puzzled by parents who volunteered time to coach sports, or raised funds for cancer research. They believed that acts of charity and community work were not supposed to flourish in a selfish capitalist society. The communist regime had not explained to these people that acts of altruism are to be expected of people who have been trained by the handling of private property to consider the consequences of their actions on others. Pareto-efficient systems run on lateral lines of cooperation, and agreement between property owners paradoxically endows a system of free trade in property with many of the imagined features of socialism.

It is in the former Soviet Union, the erstwhile flag-bearer of communism and absent property rights that social apathy reigns, charity is sparse, brutal selfishness is on display, and people live by the motto well known from communist times: "he who does not rob from the state, robs from his family." This value vacuum is a hangover from socialism which, as Paul Zak, a founder of the field of neuroeconomics, writes, provided "innumerable incentives to be non-virtuous. This lack of values is understandable when one seeks to survive, rather than thrive. Purges, gulags, and innumerable spies do not make a virtuous society." So powerful, in fact, can the effect of central control be that the effect can change people's preferences for generations. In a study entitled, *Goodbye Lenin (Or Not?)*, Alberto Alesina and Nicola Fuchs-Schündeln found that in the former East Germany, forty-five years of heavy state intervention and indoctrination

> instilled in people the view that the state is essential for individual well-being … the effects of communism are large and long lasting. It will take about one to two generations for former East and West Germans to look alike in terms of preferences and attitudes about fundamental questions regarding the role of the government in society. (page 1507)

We are only starting to build an understanding about whether property rights can reduce fundamental animosities between groups of people, yet groundbreaking research in the young field of neuroeconomics suggests there is reason for optimism. If the answer turns out to be yes, then a valuable lesson will have been learned which may help some societies to slowly dissolve the hatreds that divide them and accelerate their progress towards Pareto's Republic.

The challenge of Malthus

EVEN SOCIETIES THAT somehow manage to solve large-scale animosities within must realize they will face many economic ups and downs until they have built a foundation with private property rights and devised a style of government that provides public goods at a competitive price. That is because property rights are tools that allow people to make decisions in ways that balance social accounts. When these rights are incomplete, flawed, or nonexistent, then calculations people make in their own self-interest can push society into troubling cycles of boom and bust, as the following tale illustrates.

Writing two hundred years ago, Thomas Malthus argued that any increase in productivity that led to a multiplication of food, or clothes, or coal, would encourage people to breed. Procreation would rise to the point, he felt, where the population would be larger, but no individual member of it would be any better off than before because hungry mouths would have multiplied to devour the surplus. Before society settled down to this neutral state, it would experience periods of excessive growth in population as people bred more quickly than warranted by supplies, and periods of population decline as excess numbers perished for want of supplies or in conflicts over these supplies.

In chapter ten of the first edition of *An Essay on the Principle of Population*, Malthus speculated that the boom and bust of populations around a state of subsistence are exacerbated by a lack of property rights. Malthus did not go into details but historical research since then suggests that when people enjoyed an unexpected bounty such as a salary increase they did not have much choice in how to invest that bounty for the future. Investing in property or shares was extremely hazardous due to the still fragile nature of property rights. An attractive alternative was to convert the unexpected bounty of food into added offspring. The one investment that held hope of paying something back was to put resources into having children. Being brought up in a largely lawless society also meant that parents did not have to pay the full price of their children's upkeep. By foraging and robbing, children could maintain the caloric levels needed to survive while shifting the cost to others. This swarm of hungry waifs contributed to the overexploitation of resources which ultimately leads to the sort of general impoverishment Malthus observed. Boris Pasternak wrote of a similar scenario of need in a time of lawlessness in his native Russia. In *Doctor Zhivago*, commissar Yevgrav says, "I told myself it was beneath my dignity to arrest a man for pilfering firewood. But nothing ordered by the Party is beneath the dignity of any man. And the Party was right. One man desperate for a bit of fuel is pathetic. Five million people desperate for fuel will destroy a city."

Economists James Brander and M. Scott Taylor have produced a detailed mathematical model of Malthusian population growth in the absence of property rights and their findings do not make for happy reading. They write that,

A modern case that might be consistent with our model is Rwanda, which entered the news during 1994 because of a violent civil war. This war was normally attributed to ethnic tensions between Hutus and Tutsis, but more careful analysis suggests the possibility that Malthusian population growth, resource degradation, and resulting competition for resources was at the root of the conflict. Between 1950 and 1994, the population in Rwanda quadrupled. The boom began in the 1950s when advances in health care and agricultural practice led to increasing real incomes and rising net fertility. By the 1980s what had been an open frontier was "filled up," and real living standards started to fall. Conflict over land between Hutus and Tutsis became increasingly severe, culminating in a civil war in which a significant fraction of the population was killed. (page 134)

Political scientist Thomas Homer-Dixon's vast survey of environmental degradation and social strife in countries with insecure property rights supports Brander and Taylor's work and goes so far as to suggest that China may fall into chaos if it cannot resolve these problems. Rich countries are safe from Malthusian population cycles, in part because they have managed by tremendous effort and trial and error over centuries to establish regimes that protect property rights, but the property rights solution has brought its own form of perniciously inspired fluctuation. Any advocate of Pareto's Republic will acknowledge that to protect property rights and provide other public goods, we need government. Government must pay for property-rights-protecting services by levying taxes. Yet, as we saw in the chapter on democracy, governments can fall prey to political market failure. To enjoy the competitive drive that democracy gives to government, we must also limit terms of office. This limit means that property rights to power are short-lived, with the consequence that political groups take a short-term perspective of the taxable economic base. This base can be thought of as a common property resource, with the distinction that here the issue in contention is not a fishery or a forest, but rather the wealth government can tax.

These fiscal commons are the setting for Malthusian cycles in the economy. Every increment in private wealth generated by the creative use of property rights leads interest groups to increase their claim on the taxable base. The higher taxes that result may in turn slow the economy, which in turn may reduce interest group activity so that in the ebb, the economy recovers, thereby setting the stage for a renewed cycle. This story can be played out on many different stages and goes by a variety of names. In the animal world, biologists call it the predator-prey cycle, and have developed a complex mathematical model of how it works. Political scientist William Nordhaus and economist Alberto Alesina speak of "political business cycles" to capture the essence of these interactions between politics and the economy. Economists and public choice scholars are blunter. They speak of what Dan Usher has called "dynastic cycles" that govern the rise and fall of predatory classes. Whatever language you use, the point is similar. We live in a world of economic ups and downs created not just by chance scientific discoveries, or unexpected natural disasters, but also by the interactions of those who hold property rights and those who wish to use the force of government to enjoy the fruits of these rights.

The cycles that result from the interaction of politics and the economy should concern us, because they reflect a never-ending imbalance in social accounts that may one day become too difficult to sustain. This imbalance arises from a tragedy of the fiscal commons that provokes an over-harvesting through taxes of the economic base. The harvest is too great because those who feed upon its fruits now are not necessarily those who will pay the consequences later. The economic boom years of the 1980s led to an unprecedented rise in the size of government. Political optimism outstripped economic realism because the officials at the helm of the government juggernaut knew they would not be around later to pay for the mistaken forecasts upon which they were basing their expansion. When Western economies collapsed in the early 1990s few politicians were held to serious account. We were fortunate then because we were pulled back only two steps for the three we have taken forward in the 1980s, but the examples of Tsarist Russia, and Argentina in the 1930s give us pause. Both countries seemed on a solid path towards prosperity, yet both succumbed to struggles over the fiscal commons that plunged them into economic catastrophe lasting close to seventy years. The failure of both these great countries was one of failing to protect property.

Getting there

To SUMMARIZE THIS chapter so far, the biggest challenges to building Pareto's Republic are twofold: entrenched group hatreds and the difficulty of establishing private property rights while at the same time containing the inevitable lack of property rights over government power. I wish I could give clear instructions for bringing about changes that will resolve these challenges, but I cannot. I do not know for certain how to get to Pareto's Republic. This does not mean the place does not exist but rather that the path to it is mysterious. I can say with greater certainty that I recognize the place when I am there, and that if we at least know what our destination looks like, we will be able to tell if our path has brought us to the right place.

That place is one where control over resources is shuttled about through the exchange of property rights until the resource ends in the hands of the owner who can maximize its potential. This is what is called Pareto efficiency and it has other desirable features, such as allowing large, fast-moving societies to function with a minimum of coercion from government. The Republic is not a utopia.

Pareto efficiency cannot eliminate hostility and aggressive impulses. It can redirect them towards productive pursuits even though ill feelings between parties to an exchange may linger. How many tenants feel warmly about their landlord? How many passengers feel grateful for flying knee-to-chin on a charter flight to the Bahamas? While the peace of Pareto may be a prosperous one, it is not necessarily a loving peace. Nor is it a refuge from uncertainty. Pareto efficiency guarantees that no one who enters into an exchange believes that his or her interests are harmed at the time of the agreement. It is not a pledge that property will hold its value or that the new owner will not have a change of heart and regret a purchase. The yearning for communal life based on the older principle of the Golden Rule is evident among people who live in modern industrialized societies. Perhaps Pareto's Republic is only a stop on the way to some future, very different form of social organization.

No matter what the future holds, at present, Pareto's Republic produces the richest, healthiest, and safest environment in which to live and is the source of almost all the world's scientific discovery and artistic exploration. Yet the difficulties of building the Republic are so great in most countries, and progress so slow, that hundreds of millions of people who live outside its confines try to immigrate to countries that are based on property rights and the rule of law, the vectors of Pareto-efficiency. It is almost unheard of for anyone to leave the Republic to live in countries where the law of the strong prevails and resources are the cause of unending struggles that make people quite tired of their lives.

If history is a guide, then the answer to reaching Pareto's Republic may lie in these huge international migrations. As the example of Europe roughly four hundred years ago showed, usually the most highly trained and productive people are the ones to leave their countries, creating a brain drain to nations that are based on property rights, thereby enriching them and impoverishing the countries left behind. If the leaders of countries left behind persist in their morbid nostalgia for retrograde governments based on theft, then sooner or later they will be invaded or bullied by neighbours, thereby sending a cautionary message to other countries that fail to reform. A less drastic development will be that the elites of inefficient countries will simply sell their power to international conglomerates. Something like this is happening in parts of the Congo and Angola, where China has leased vast tracts of mineral and agricultural properties the size of small countries. Under the protection of security forces they have imported, the Chinese are regularizing the exploitation of these resources and perhaps laying the basis for rule of law once the leases expire.

For the competitive strain of international migrations to have a fruitful effect on governments that resist reform, some model on which to base it is needed. The model I have proposed in this book is based on Pareto's definition of economic efficiency and is the result of several decades of research by thinkers from many fields who, I believe, are creating a new science of peace. Of course, the model is an ideal. Even countries that have had the greatest success in establishing property rights never quite live in the Republic of Pareto, but just pitch their tents in one of its proverbial suburbs. The Republic is like a rainbow whose arc we follow with varying degrees of success. Where is the pot of gold at the end? I suspect the answer to that question does not really matter. What matters is that we try to emulate the Republic and that through our efforts we strive to convert our antagonisms into something fruitful. That sort of peace is the real treasure we gain from believing in and working out the details of Pareto's Republic.

READINGS 8

Abrams, Burton A. and Russell F. Settle (1978). "The Economic Theory of Regulation and Public Financing of Presidential Elections." Pages 245–257 in *The Journal of Political Economy*. Volume 86.

Alchian, Armen A. (1950). "Uncertainty, Evolution, and Economic Theory." Pages 211–221 in *The Journal of Political Economy*. Volume 58.

Alesina, Alberto (1988). "Macroeconomics and politics" Pages 13–52 in *NBER Macroeconomics Annual*. Edited by Olivier Blanchard and S. Fischer. MIT Press.

Alesina, Alberto and Nicola Fuchs-Schündeln (2007). "Good-bye Lenin (or not?): the effect of Communism on people's preferences." Pages 1507–1528 in the *American Economic Review*. Volume 97.

Becker, Gary S. (1958). "Competition and Democracy." *Journal of Law and Economics*. Volume 1.

Becker, Gary S. (1971). *The economics of discrimination*. University of Chicago Press.

Becker, Gary S. and Casey B. Mulligan (2003). "Deadweight Costs and the Size of Government." Pages 293–340 in the *Journal of Law and Economics*. Volume 46.

Black, Duncan (1948). "On the Rationale of Group Decision-making." Pages 23–34 in *The Journal of Political Economy*. Volume 56.

Blaug, Mark (2007). "The Fundamental Theorems of Modern Welfare Economics, Historically Contemplated." Pages 185–207 in *History of Political Economy*. Volume 39.

Brander, James A. and M. Scott Taylor (1998). "The Simple Economics of Easter Island: A Ricardo-Malthus Model of Renewable Resource Use." Pages 119–138 in *The American Economic Review*. Volume 88.

Buchanan, Allen (1985). *Ethics, efficiency, and the market*. Rowman & Allanheld.

Buchanan, James (1988). "Contractarian political economy and constitutional interpretation." Pages 135–139 in the *American Economic Review*. Volume 78.

Buchanan, James M. and Gordon Tullock (1962). T*he calculus of consent: logical foundations of constitutional democracy*. University of Michigan Press.

Buchanan, James M. and Geoffrey Brennan (1980). *The power to tax: analytical foundations of a fiscal constitution*. Cambridge University Press.

Caruso, Raul (2010). "On the Nature of Peace Economics." Article 2 in Issue 2 of *Peace Economics, Peace Science and Public Policy*: Volume 16.

Chipman, John S. (1998). "The Contributions of Ragnar Frisch to Economics and Econometrics." Pages 58–110 *Econometrics and Economic Theory in the 20th Century: The Ragnar Frisch Centennial Symposium*. Edited by Steinar Strom. Cambridge University Press.

Chipman, John S. (2006). "Pareto and contemporary economic theory." Pages 451–475 in the *International Review of Economics*. Volume 53.

Cipolla, Carlo M. (1976). *Before the industrial revolution: European society and economy, 1000-1700*. Norton & Company.

Coase, Ronald. H. (1937). "The Nature of the Firm." Pages 386–405 in *Economica*. Volume 4.

Demsetz, Harold (1967). "Toward a theory of property rights." Pages 347–359 in *The American Economic Review*. Volume 57.

Demsetz, Harold (2002). "Toward a Theory of Property Rights II: The Competition between Private and Collective Ownership." Pages s653–s672 in *The Journal of Legal Studies*. Volume 31.

Dixit, Avinash K. (2004). *Lawlessness and Economics: Alternative Modes of Governance*. Princeton University Press.

Domar, Evsey D. (1989). *Capitalism, Socialism and Serfdom: Essays by Evsey D. Domar*. Cambridge University Press.

Easton, Stephen T. and Michael Walker (1992). *Rating global economic freedom*. Fraser Institute.

Frey, Bruno S. and Benno Torgler (2007). "Tax morale and conditional cooperation." Pages 136–159 in the *Journal of Comparative Economics*. Volume 35.

Gordon, H. Scott (1954). "The Economic Theory of a Common-Property Resource: The Fishery." Pages 124–142 in *The Journal of Political Economy*. Volume 62.

Gwartney, James, Randall Holcombe, and Robert Lawson (1998). "The scope of government and the wealth of nations." Pages 163–190 in the *Cato Journal*. Volume 18.

Gwartney, James, Joshua Hall, and Robert Lawson (2010). *Economic freedom of the world 2010: annual report*. Fraser Institute.

Harberger, Arnold C. (1964). "The Measurement of Waste." Pages 58–76 in *The American Economic Review*. Volume 54.

Hardin, Garrett (1968). "The Tragedy of the Commons." Pages 1243–1248 in *Science*. Volume 162.

Hayek, Friedrich August (1945). "The use of knowledge in society." Pages 519–530 in *The American Economic Review*. Volume 35.

Hayek, Friedrich August (1989). "The pretence of knowledge." Pages 3–7 in T*he American Economic Review*, Vol. 79.

Heilbroner, Robert (1992). *Twenty-first century capitalism*. House of Anansi Press.

Hicks, John (1939). "The Foundations of Welfare Economics." Pages 696–712 in the *Economic Journal*. Volume 69.

Homer-Dixon, Thomas F. (1994). "Environmental Scarcities and Violent Conflict: Evidence from Cases." Pages 5–40 in *International Security*. Volume 19.

Hovenkamp, Herbert (2010). "Coase, Institutionalism, and the Origins of Law and Economics." Pages 499–542 in the *Indiana Law Journal*. Volume 86.

Kaldor, Nicholas (1939). "Welfare Propositions in Economics and Interpersonal Comparisons of Utility." Pages 549–552 in the *Economic Journal*. Volume 69.

Lange, Oscar (1936). "On the economic theory of socialism: Part I." Pages 53–71 in the *Review of Economic Studies*. Volume 4.

Lange, Oscar (1942). "The Foundations of Welfare Economics." Pages 215–228 in *Econometrica*. Volume 10.

Lipsey, Richard G, and Kelvin Lancaster (1956). "The General Theory of Second Best." Pages 11–32 in *The Review of Economic Studies*. Volume 24.

Malthus, Thomas Robert (1798). *An Essay on the Principle of Population*. Library of Economics and Liberty. Available at http://www.econlib.org/library/Malthus/malPop.html

Marlow, Michael L. (2000). "Spending, school structure, and public education quality: evidence from California." Pages 89–106 in the *Economics of Education Review*. Volume 19.

Matsusaka, John G. (2008). *For the Many or the Few: The Initiative, Public Policy, and American Democracy.* University Of Chicago Press.

McNeill, William H. (1963). *The Rise of the West: A History of the Human Community.* University of Chicago Press.

McNeill, William H. (1976). *Plagues and Peoples.* Anchor Press/Doubleday.

McNeill, William H. (1984). *The Pursuit of Power: Technology, Armed Force, and Society since A.D. 1000.* University Of Chicago Press.

Mueller, Dennis C. (2003). *Public Choice III.* Cambridge University Press.

Murphy, Kevin M., Andrei Shleifer, and Robert W. Vishny (1991). "The allocation of talent: implications for growth." Pages 503–530 in *The Quarterly Journal of Economics*, Volume 106.

Murphy, Kevin M., Andrei Shleifer, and Robert W. Vishny (1993). "Why Is Rent-Seeking So Costly to Growth?" Pages 409–414 in *The American Economic Review*. Volume 83.

Murshed, Syed Mansoob (2010). "On the Salience of Identity in Civilizational and Sectarian Conflict." Article 9 in Issue 2 of *Peace Economics, Peace Science and Public Policy*. Volume 16.

Musgrave, Richard Abel (1959). *The theory of public finance: a study in public economy.* McGraw-Hill.

Nordhaus, William (1989). "Alternative approaches to the political business cycle." Pages 1–68 in the *Brookings Papers on Economic Activity*. Volume 2.

North, Douglass Cecil (1990). *Institutions, institutional change, and economic performance.* Cambridge University Press.

Olson, Mancur (1982). *The Rise and Decline of Nations: Economic Growth, Stagflation, and Social Rigidities.* Yale University Press.

Ostrom, Elinor (2010). "Beyond Markets and States: Polycentric Governance of Complex Economic Systems." Pages 641–672 in the *American Economic Review*. Volume 100.

Palda, Filip(1992). "Desirability and effects of campaign spending limits." Pages 295–317 in *Crime, Law and Social Change*. Volume 21.

Popper, Karl (1945). *The open society and its enemies: the spell of Plato*. Routledge.

Rauch, James E. (2005). "Getting the Properties Right to Secure Property Rights: Dixit's Lawlessness and Economics." Pages 480–487 in the *Journal of Economic Literature*. Volume XLIII.

Romer, Paul M. (2008) "Economic Growth." *The Concise Encyclopedia of Economics*. 2008. Library of Economics and Liberty. Available at http://www.econlib.org/library/Enc/EconomicGrowth.html

Rosen, Sherwin (1974). "Hedonic Prices and Implicit Markets: Product Differentiation in Pure Competition." Pages 34–55 in *The Journal of Political Economy*. Volume 82.

Rostow, Walt Whitman. *The Stages of Economic Growth: A Non-Communist Manifesto*. Cambridge University Press (1960)

Rowley, Charles K. (2004). "Political Business Cycles." Pages 3–31 in *The Encyclopedia of Public Choice Volume I*. Edited by Charles K. Rowley and Friedrich Schneider. Kluwer Academic Publishers.

Ruff, Julius Ralph (2001). *Violence in early modern Europe, 1500–1800*. Cambridge University Press.

Schultz, Henry (1928). "Reviewed work(s): Vilfredo Pareto: Sa Vie et Son Oeuvre by G. H. Bousquet." Pages 740–742 in *The Journal of Political Economy*. Volume 36.

Schumpeter Joseph A. (1943). *Capitalism, socialism and democracy*. George Allen and Unwin.

Stigler, George J. (1992). "Law or Economics?" Pages 455–468 in the *Journal of Law and Economics*. Volume 35.

Stiglitz, Joseph E. (1987). "Pareto efficient and optimal taxation and the new new welfare economics." Pages 991–1042 in the *Handbook of Public Economics Volume II*. Edited by Alan J. Auerbach and Martin Feldstein. Elsevier Science Publishers B.V. (North-Holland).

Tanzi, Vito and Ludger Schuknecht (1997). "Reconsidering the Fiscal Role of Government: The International Perspective." Pages 164–168 in *The American Economic Review*. Volume 87.

De Tocqueville, Alexis (2009). "Letters from America." *The Hudson Review*. Autumn 2009: Volume 3.

Usher, Dan (1981). *The Economic Prerequisites to Democracy*. Blackwell.

Usher, Dan (1989). "The Dynastic Cycle and the Stationary State." Pages 1031–1044 in *The American Economic Review. Volume 79*.

Willett, Thomas D. and Mandfred W. Keil (2003). "Political Business Cycles." Pages 411–415 in *The Encyclopedia of Public Choice Volume II*. Edited by Charles K. Rowley and Friedrich Schneider. Kluwer Academic Publishers.

Wittfogel, Karl A. (1981). *Oriental despotism: A comparative study of total power*. Vintage Books.

Zak, Paul J. (2008). "Introduction." Pages xi to xxii in *Moral Markets: The Critical Role of Values in the Economy*. Edited by Paul J. Zak and Michael C. Jense. Princeton University Press.